T5-CUU-017

DAUGHTERS OF EVE

GAMALIEL BRADFORD

DAUGHTERS OF EVE

The New Home Library
NEW YORK

THE NEW HOME LIBRARY EDITION PUBLISHED OCTOBER, 1942
BY ARRANGEMENT WITH HOUGHTON MIFFLIN COMPANY
REPRINTED DECEMBER, 1942
REPRINTED FEBRUARY, 1943

THE NEW HOME LIBRARY, 14 West Forty-ninth Street
New York, N. Y.

CL

PRINTED IN THE UNITED STATES OF AMERICA

TO
LYTTON STRACHEY
WHO MAKES BIOGRAPHY
NOT ONLY A CURIOUS SCIENCE
BUT AN EXQUISITE ART

"Who is't can read a woman?"
CYMBELINE

CONTENTS

DAUGHTERS OF EVE

I

EVE IN THE APPLE-ORCHARD
NINON DE LENCLOS

CHRONOLOGY

Anne de Lenclos.
Born, Paris, November, 1620.
Father died, 1641.
Mother died, 1643.
Affair with Villarceaux, 1652.
Settled in Rue des Tournelles about 1667.
Died, Paris, October 17, 1705.

DAUGHTERS OF EVE

I

NINON DE LENCLOS

I

THREE hundred years ago Ninon de Lenclos was just such a girl as New York breeds to-day by dozens, fearing neither God nor man, daring everything, challenging everything, perfectly reckless of the tattered conventions of a worn-out morality, mocking the tame taboos of a more timid generation, determined to give full development and outlet to every power and vigor of the spirit, to suck from life every drop of rich and varied sweetness that it can possibly be made to yield.

The long life of Ninon, or, as she was christened, Anne de Lenclos, was contemporary with almost the entire sixteenth century. Born in Paris in 1620, she died there in 1705, and during that time she was intimate with many of the most prominent people in France. Some of the greatest men were her lovers, some of the most interesting women were her devoted friends. At an early period she set out to follow her own nature, as she saw it, not showing her respect for the conventions of the world by an idle battle against them, but simply disregarding them to seek a higher and a truer law. Perhaps she never found such, but at any rate she had an inborn instinct of reason and common sense which kept her head steady through the wildest excesses and enabled her after a youth of mad riot to develop an old age of dignity, tranquillity, and peace.

Naturally much that is reported about Ninon's childhood and early years is more or less legendary. But it is clear that her spiritual revolt began when she was very young. Her social position was fairly good. Her mother was timid, conservative, and pious, and was anxious to make the daughter more so, but her father was reckless, careless, dissipated, a lover of life and laughter and especially of song. It was easy to divine which of her parents Ninon's temperament would follow.

The story goes that one day when she went with her mother to church and the priests were chanting the solemn passion music, the child burst out with the refrain of a popular love-song,

> Why should we care if we die,
> When we die but to live again?

The congregation were scandalized, the mother was ready to sink with shame, and the priests labored to convert the little heathen — quite in vain. All they could get out of her was, 'What you priests tell us is sheer nonsense. I don't believe a single word of it.' [1]

She not only reflected freely and fearlessly on the things of the other world, but, what was practically more important, she formed her own ideas on the affairs of this world and especially on the conduct of men and women. Just when she framed her views on such subjects it is of course impossible to say, but according to the report of the Abbé de Châteauneuf the views were formulated early, were explicit and definite, and served as a rule of life forever after. 'As the first use she made of her reason was to free herself from vulgar errors, she early understood that there can be only one law of morals for men and for women.' [2] Which sounds surprisingly like the twentieth — and some other — centuries. What is interesting about Ninon is that she tried to apply the principle from every point of view, that is, she not only believed that women had a right to the same sexual liberty as men, but she believed that they should recognize equally with men all the obligations of loyalty, sincerity, and honor, and she made a conscientious effort to put this belief into practice in her own case.

Her experiments may not have been always in every way successful. She may have overlooked some differences in the training and surroundings of women which tend to make their lapses more serious and more offensive — to men — than those of the corresponding masculine article. At any rate, the experiment was profoundly interesting.

It is of course not to be supposed that a young girl could work out such ideas from her own un-aided brain. We have seen that Ninon's father had an immense influence upon her, perhaps all the more because they were early separated by his exile for an unfortunate duel. Her father set her to reading Montaigne, and it is easy to imagine the effect of Montaigne's sceptical naturalism on a temperament like hers, at once infinitely bold and infinitely pleasure-loving. It was not Montaigne alone. She read all sorts of books, probably with little system or profound or persistent erudition, but with that extraordinarily quick and ready wit which enabled her to seize the essential in things and people and always adapt it to her purposes. When she discusses love, she can quote a Greek poet or philosopher. When she attacks theology, she has a church father ready to her hand. She probably knew very little about either fathers or philosophers, but she knew enough to serve her end, and she was admirably prompt and eager in the use of it, as she was in everything.

She kept in touch not only with dead authors but with the living. The very greatest author living in her day was Molière, and if we may trust tradition, Molière used to read his plays to her and take her advice about them. According to Châteauneuf, when the dramatist read her his 'Tartufe,' she matched it with an anecdote told 'with color so lively and so natural that if his play had not been completed, he would never have undertaken it, for he felt incapable of putting on the stage anything so perfect as the Tartufe of Ninon.' [3]

However this may be, it is clear that Ninon's liberty was quite as much intellectual as moral and that her independence of conduct had the independence of clear, consistent, and vigorous thinking behind it. Indeed in her old age she reminds one of her lovers that he used to make fun of her for thinking so deeply, and it is evident that the profound and searching possibilities of thought were never alien to her.

But from any danger of excessive reflection, or of brooding analysis or melancholy, Ninon was easily saved by her intensely social instincts. She wanted people about her, all sorts of people. If there were deep questions to be thought of, she wanted to talk them over with wise and liberal friends. She had scholars for scholarship and authors for literature and unlimited clever abbés for theology. And she was just as ready for the lighter side of talk also. Her wit was as ready as her brain was keen. Innumerable quick touches and vivid repartees of hers have been handed down through the years, some doubtless invented, and some, as it appears to us, rather trivial and pointless, as is so often the case with reported wit, but many sharp and eminently significant, like her swift retort, when some one expressed astonishment at her having so long kept her beauty, 'it is because I have never cared for cards or wine or women,' [4] or her apt quotation of Corneille to the pompous marshal, who was pressing a hopeless suit and incidentally praising his own good qualities,

Oh, Ciel! que de vertus vous me faites haïr! [5]

And to the constant readiness to see the humorous side of others she added the charming gift which redeems this from acidity, the readiness to make fun of herself.

The sense of fun, of comedy, was even pushed to folly, to lighter trifling, to jests and practical jokes

8

of every sort. But there is a notable insistence that with Ninon the most extreme fooling was not allowed to pass the bounds of good taste. The wildest young nobles of the court might visit her when they pleased, but if they did visit her she insisted upon respect and manners with her as decorous as with the Queen.

For it is evident that in everything the woman was an artist, and her latest biographer justly insists that she instinctively made life a fine art.[6] There is something Greek about her, something Attic, in her sense of restraint and delicacy, even in indulgence, even in encroaching excess. She suggests the best type of Greek courtesan, Lais, or the charming Leontium of Epicurus and Landor's Dialogue, or even the Aspasia of Pericles. She had the finest sensibility to beauty in every form, and expecially in the most æsthetic form of all, music. How subtle is Châteauneuf's description of its effect upon her: 'You followed in her face the different emotions and passions that the musician was trying to express, for she found expression where we should find only harmony, and you would have said that to her every sound was a feeling.'[7]

The only aspect of beauty that I do not find registered in connection with Ninon is the appreciation of Nature. But I feel confident that one who was so alive to the depths and possibilities of reflection must have been capable of enjoying solitary walks in wide fields and deep woods as much as Madame de Sévigné enjoyed them.

In the same way you feel, or perhaps rather divine, in Ninon the capacity for religious emotion, in spite of her violent outbursts of irreligion. She had queer spells of devotional tendency, which filter down to us through the dimness of biographical record. After her mother's death she had a time of depression which took her to a convent. Again she sought another such refuge during a sojourn in Lyon. And still again she was actually incarcerated for a time by the order of the Queen, Anne of Austria. You would naturally say that a temperament so quick and so responsive would feel at least the possibilities of God. But somehow when it came to actual conventual surroundings, Ninon's religion was all dissolved in her humanity. She won the enthusiastic affection of the nuns first, and then gradually a swarm of outside people — women and those fatal men — began to buzz about her, and God was easily and deplorably forgotten.

For she was a creature of this world all over, and the human touch was essential and on the whole sufficient for her, as it was for her close contemporary, Madame de Sévigné, who was so different in many ways and yet so obviously sympathetic and admiring on the few occasions when they were brought near each other. They were both thorough children of the Renaissance, that period of magnificent this-worldliness, which is rampant in Montaigne and the painting of Rubens, but reaches its highest manifestation, for us English-speaking people at any rate, in the drama of Shakespeare and his fellows. The splendor and richness of this world have never been better developed and exemplified than in the horde and herd of Shakespeare's men and women, and Ninon, who was a true cousin of Madame de Sévigné, was also a cousin, a creature, a real daughter, of Shakespeare, and one he would hardly have been ashamed to own.

II

Certainly the most intense, if not the most profound or enduring, of the aspects of humanness is the aspect of sex, and it must be admitted that sex played a showy and conspicuous part in the career of Ninon de Lenclos. One asks oneself first, had she the beauty to justify this? As in many such cases, the actual portraits are not very satisfactory. There is a suggestion of rich voluptuousness, but also of heaviness, which does not greatly attract. The printed descriptions are better and give more of charm. Thus, in Scudéry's 'Clélie' Ninon is pictured as the heroine: 'Her hair is of the most beautiful chestnut brown that ever was seen, the face is round, the coloring brilliant, the mouth agreeable, the lips very red, there is a little dimple in the chin, which is infinitely becoming, the black eyes are shining, full of fire and laughter, and the whole face is delicate, gay, and keenly intelligent.' [8] But somehow this detailed analysis does not begin to give the charm of mobility and responsiveness that appear in another description by a contemporary: 'Her countenance was at once open, delicate, fine, tender, and animated. When nothing especially affected her and in the daily course of life, she appeared cold and indifferent; but when even a petty incident roused her spirit from this state of repose, which the multiplicity of her emotions seemed to render necessary to her, her whole person was transformed: her features were touched with passion, the sound of her voice went to the heart, the grace of her gestures and of her poses, everything about her charmed the feelings and stimulated them to the highest degree.' [9]

In any case, there can be no question but that
Ninon made good use of her charms, such as they
were, and got out of them all they would yield in
an amorous career of extraordinary brilliancy and
variety, and especially of extraordinary length. It
was even said that she charmed the Sévignés of
three generations, though in the last case the charm
was no doubt of a social and maternal order, as
with the legendary adventure of the Abbé Gédoyn,
when the lady was eighty years old. The list of
lovers as a whole, however, was anything but
legendary. There were men of business and men of
pleasure, men of the sword and men of the church,
scholars, authors, and philosophers, men handsome
and ugly. Their names are largely recorded in the
scandalous chronicles of the time and need not concern us here.

But two general points in connection with this
eminently disreputable list deserve to be noted.
First, there is the delicate question of money.
There can be no doubt that Ninon took from her
lovers, took largely as she spent freely, and used
her prudent foresight to accumulate wisely for
more barren years. But she never gave her favor
for money alone. She demanded other things with
it, and she could and did refuse gifts, even magnifi-

cent, when the giver did not please her. Second, she exercised her privilege of rejection at all times. She loved only those who she at least thought deserved her love in some way, and if you did not deserve it, you might beg and sue and plead and pay as long as you pleased, you made no impression whatever. She herself laughingly divided her lovers into payers, martyrs, and favorites, and the martyrs had a hard time of it.

In all this wide and erratic amorousness the chief and prevalent note is gayety and mirth. Ninon refused to take love as a serious thing. Her vast experience of the world, and especially of men, had taught her, or she thought it had, that a man's passion was brief, however ardent, and the more ardent, the briefer. You should taste it, and savor it, and fling it away, and forget it. Otherwise you ran extreme risk of being flung away and forgotten yourself, and this risk she proposed to avoid. Love was an exquisite trifle, it was no more, and her way was to treat it as such. Therefore her path was strewn with roses and laughter, and she is the center of a garland of gay anecdotes, some trivial, some dubious, but all merry and light-hearted, and none really cynical or cruel. Perhaps a rejected lover hurled his scorn at her in verse:

'Unworthy of my sighs and tears,
I see at last that I was mad:
My love bestowed, it now appears,
Ungrateful, charms you never had,'

and instantly she could toss him back:

'Unmoved I see your passion go,
And know that you have loved it through.
If love has charms it can bestow,
Why not bestow them upon you?' [10]

Or, there is the story of the weary lover who fell asleep while expecting his lady's arrival. Ninon crept into his room, stole his garments and his sword, and the next morning burst in upon him in mannish attire, with the sword at her side, and threatened his life. And there is the excellent, undying jest of La Châtre. This La Châtre was a grave and serious gentleman, who was obliged to part from his lady for a short journey and begged her to give him a written pledge of fidelity to carry with him. Ninon looked at him for a moment, with a whimsical gravity, which he should have fathomed, said nothing, but signed his paper. No sooner was he gone than she sought lovers where she could, and with every one of them she broke out into a burst of laughter: 'Oh, that delightful guarantee I gave La Châtre!' The story went all over France, all over the world, and poor La

Châtre has been a laughing-stock for ten generations.

One asks oneself whether the laughter was really all, and whether even Ninon did not have her moments when love unveiled its deeper secrets and passion its mysteries and despairs. Surely no one would have been more capable of understanding them than she. The delicate analysis of the subject in her brilliant little story 'La Coquette Vengée' would seem to suggest something of the kind, and even, in referring to the misery of another, she is said to have observed that 'matters of tenderness produce more of suffering than they can ever give of joy.' [11] There are rare hints of jealousy, also, and it might be possible to find an occasional suggestion of satiety or disgust. Above all, in one instance love seems to have taken a deeper hold. Whereas most of her fancies were brief, and she herself designated them as caprices, light and whiffling breezes that merely fluttered the rippling surface of her soul, she did have an affair with the Marquis de Villarceaux, which lasted three years, apparently with a notable and romantic fidelity. It is in connection with him that the pretty story is told that, when he thought he had occasion for jealousy, Ninon cut off all her beautiful hair and sent it to him as a token that she was constant. The details of their parting are obscure, but would seem to have more elements of tragedy in them than Ninon commonly allowed to disfigure or transfigure her affections.

If this was so, she had learned her lesson, and she did not permit it to sour or embitter her life. Once more and more than ever, she determined to identify love with laughter and with song. So taken, it could be made the grace and ornament and charm of existence. Wreathe smiles and jests and good-nature about it. Fill it full with light airs and merry, lilting verses. In other words, make it your servant, not your master, and it will serve you with grace and delicacy and delight. If she had known them, I am sure she would have reveled in the mirth and magic of the great Shakespearean love-song of the world,

> What is love? 'Tis not hereafter.
> Present mirth hath present laughter;
> What's to come is still unsure.
> In delay there lies no plenty;
> Then come kiss me, Sweet and Twenty,
> Youth's a stuff will not endure.

III

But at an early period of her career Ninon made up her mind that while love might be worth trifling with, there were other matters that demanded more serious thought, things that did endure, the solid loyalty of affection, the assured and lasting comfort of mutual understanding. She always honestly and earnestly insisted on her principle, that if women were to have masculine privileges, they should also fully recognize masculine duties, and it is said that her daily prayer was, 'Mon Dieu, faites de moi un honnête homme et n'en faites jamais une honnête femme,' 'Dear God, make me a good man, but never a good woman,' [12] The delicate observation of La Bruyère, 'A lovely woman who has the qualities of an honest man is the most delicious character in the world, you find in her all the merit of both sexes,' [13] is said to have been made with reference to Ninon de Lenclos.

This charming loyalty and fidelity is obvious in all the aspects of Ninon's human dealing. It shows in her relations with her family. To be sure, as happens in so many cases, she and her mother did not quite understand each other. The mother was timid, Ninon was daring; Ninon lived for this world, her mother for the next. Yet in her mother's final illness no daughter could have been more devoted, and the mother's death was for the time a cause of acute distress.

With the father there was more natural sympathy.

We have seen that to his early suggestions Ninon owed much of her general attitude toward life, and the sympathy was probably by no means diminished by the father's years of exile. When he returned to die in his daughter's arms, the words attributed to him on his deathbed are a perfect epitome of the daughter's apparent philosophy of life: 'You see that all that remains to me at this moment is the dreary memory of pleasures that are quitting me. Their possession has been fleeting and that is all I have to complain of.... But you, who are to survive me, profit by the precious time and be scrupulous not so much about the number as about the choice of your pleasures.' [14]

The glimpses we get of Ninon as a mother are vague and elusive, culminating in the legend of the son who made love to her in her later years and was driven to suicide when he discovered his horrible mistake. But the correspondence in which she appeals to a high functionary for financial and professional assistance for the boy who was an officer in the navy has all the dignity and courtesy of an honest man and all the tenderness of a good woman.

Ninon appears to have been equally gracious and considerate with those who served her and to have been correspondingly beloved by them. In the will that disposed of her moderate possessions she left six thousand francs in different sums to her various domestics.

In money matters generally there was the same kindly wisdom and the same practical business sense. Ninon did not care greatly for either the riches or the honors of the world, at least did not care enough to make sacrifices for them. Perhaps if she had been willing to take the trouble, she might have climbed as high as her intimate friend Madame de Maintenon, have been the mistress of a king, or at least the lady of a great estate. She knew too well the burden of these things, as Madame de Maintenon came to find it. She believed in supplying the necessary, but not the superfluous, and she knew that the really exquisite things of life cannot be supplied by prevision at all. In one of those touches of delicate insight that are so characteristic of her she sums up this view: 'We should take care to lay in a stock of provisions, but not of pleasures: these should be gathered day by day.' [15]

Nevertheless, in all her financial concerns she was thrifty and careful. She did not want riches, she did want independence, and to secure comfort and freedom in her old age. Therefore she administered her little patrimony and her savings with shrewd discretion and had enough put by for any number of rainy days that might occur.

As to spending she was equally provident. She was simple in all her tastes. She prided herself on keeping a good appetite till age, but it was because she had always eaten temperately. In the same way she rarely touched alcohol. With her natural vivacity it was not needed, since it was said of her that she was intoxicated from the first taste of soup. But she abhorred a drunkard and would have nothing to do with one. Her dress was as unpretentious as her food: no display, no extravagance, 'costly garments did not suit her, but what was always of the most elegant simplicity and the most exquisite freshness.' [16]

Though she was careful and frugal, she could, however, spend freely when the whim took her, and above all she was generous. When a friend was in trouble and wanted money, others might fail him, not Ninon. She was not only willing, she was usually able, which is less common, and her prudent habits ensured a stock of funds that could be called on at need.

The masculine business habits involved not only generosity but reliability and the certainty of response to obligations that had been incurred perhaps a long time before. There may be some legendary amplifications in the story of Gourville, but confirmatory evidence substantiates the general drift of it. This Gourville was obliged to quit Paris for a time, and, not wishing to take his money with him, left half of it in deposit with a clerical friend and half with Ninon. When he returned, he went at once to the priest, but there was delay and haggling and difficulty. If the Church would not pay up, what likelihood was there that anything could be got from such a one as Ninon? Nevertheless, Gourville went to her. Ninon quietly turned to her strong box and counted out the money, which was probably her idea of praying daily to be a good man. It may have been God's idea too.

The loyalty was not merely financial, and Ninon, who flitted from one lover to another with the utmost lightness, never betrayed, never deserted, never forgot a friend. The consequence was that she had friends, men and women both, in all classes of society, who were equally devoted to her and were as ready to do her service as the world ever allows, which was probably all that Ninon ever expected. Queen Christina of Sweden visited her when she was shut up in the convent and sent word to Cardinal Mazarin that the Court lacked its greatest ornament since Ninon was not there.[17] Madame de Maintenon, who in her early years of poverty had lived in the closest intimacy with Ninon, never lost her affection for her, and would have bestowed gifts and honors upon her, if Ninon had cared to receive them.

What drew people to Ninon was not only her loyalty and fidelity, but the social grace and charm which I have already indicated and emphasized. It was her wit, her vivacity, her unfailing high spirits, and underneath these lay a profound, spontaneous appreciation and enjoyment of life, such as she herself expressed in one of her exquisite flashes of insight when she said, 'La joie de l'esprit en marque la force,' 'The joy of a soul is the measure of its force.' [18] Ninon had a gift for receiving joy as rich as her capacity for imparting it.

The interesting point is that with all the wit and all the merriment and all the keen sense of the humorous side of things, which so often estranges the foolish and disconcerts the proud, Ninon never lost a friend. One who keenly appreciated the sharpness of her sallies and the point of her satire makes this assertion with full knowledge of the facts.[19] And the explanation is obvious, that underneath all the mirth and laughter there lay still

deeper a wealth of tenderness and human understanding and sympathy, such as appears in another
of her golden phrases: 'I believe that I go further
than most people do in everything that touches the
heart.' [20] She touched hearts because she naturally
loved them, because she turned to them with
sympathetic curiosity and handled them with a
gentle and affectionate touch and found in them no
weakness and no folly that she could not parallel in
her own. In consequence she had the rare and
delightful faculty of appealing to other generations
as well as to her contemporaries, and young people
turned to her more readily for sympathy than even
to those of their own day and type. Altogether it
must be recognized that few men or women have
been more widely and heartily beloved.

IV

Thus, it would appear that some of the accepted
conventions of morality are pretty thoroughly con-
tradicted in the case of Ninon de Lenclos. After a
youth of riot and excess and wild license like hers,
she should have had nothing but a decayed and de-
graded and disreputable old age. Instead of this,
she passed all her later years sweetly, serenely, and
with the consideration, admiration, and respect of

the best people of her time. Only, as Sainte-Beuve justly points out, her case must by no means be taken as typical. There is not one young girl in a thousand who could start as Ninon did and end as she did, who would have the sanity and sense and judgment and calm vision of future possibilities to steer through so many perils and difficulties to a final port of peace.

But Ninon unquestionably did it. When she was getting toward fifty, she settled herself in a modest house, with a modest, dignified establishment, and there she passed her remaining years in a noble and cultivated leisure, seeing what was best worth seeing in the whole Parisian world. The testimony as to her conduct and her standing during these years is too general and too solid to be for a moment disputed. Madame de Sévigné, whose husband and son both had hard work to escape from Ninon's early snares, writes of her later popularity, 'The women run after Mademoiselle de Lenclos as the men used to do,' [21] and again, 'Corbinelli tells me wonders of the good company that he finds with Mademoiselle de Lenclos, in her old age she gets together everybody.' [22]

Perhaps the most enthusiastic witness is the Abbé Fraguier: 'The old loved her from their memory of her past, but not so much from the memory of her charms as of her virtues. The young loved her for the grace and the beauty they still saw in her.... It was her fortune to draw to herself the most worthy people of the Court and of the City, but she drew only the worthy... and no one would have forgiven himself for wounding her in anything. There grew up a natural bond, an intimate friendship, among all those who were intimate with her: they esteemed and loved each other naturally on that account.' [23] And if the ardor of this praise sounds a little suspicious, one can turn to the supreme recorder, the profoundest analyst of human nature, Saint-Simon, who spared no fault and overlooked no weakness, though his pen was equally powerful with grace and charm. Saint-Simon says of Ninon's social circle: 'She thus had for friends all that was most select and most lofty in the Court, so that it became the fashion to be received by her.... There was never any gambling, or loud laughter, or disputes, or arguments on religion or politics, but a great deal of wit, of the most delicate quality, old and new anecdotes, bits of charming gossip, but without ever a trace of unkindliness.... Ninon's conversation was delightful. She was disinterested, reliable, secret, could be counted upon to the very last.... And all these qualities gained her a reputation and a consideration that were altogether unusual.' [24]

But the crowning document in regard to Ninon's old age is her correspondence with Saint-Évremond, which, though much too brief, remains one of the delightful and significant epistolary exchanges of the world. Saint-Évremond himself was peculiarly fitted to understand Ninon and to enter into her view of life and attitude towards it. He had been a casual lover in the early days, but he was early and late an attached and sympathetic friend. He himself had destroyed his political career by an indiscretion and had been obliged to seek refuge in England, where he remained until his death, a shrewd, philosophical observer of human nature, his own as well as others. Sainte-Beuve, who found in him a sympathetic spirit, has analyzed both his character and his relation to Ninon with delicate skill, and no one has better appraised the fine qualities of both. Saint-Évremond's broad, sceptical insight and his sympathetic humanity are well shown in his comment on belief and unbelief, which illuminates so much of Ninon's attitude as well as of his own: 'The most devout cannot succeed in believing at all times, nor the most profane in always disbelieving, and it is one of the miseries of this life that we can have no assured reliance upon another.' [25] Perhaps he might have added that it is the supreme misery.

There is no more attractive portrayal of Ninon than that which appears in the letters written to her by Saint-Évremond. To be sure, there is at times a certain exaggeration of compliment, making the tone less genuine than that of the letters of Ninon herself, but in the main it is obvious that Saint-Évremond's attachment and respect are as profound as they are lasting. How delicate is his penetration of her character in the remark, 'If I had been told you had become devout, I should have believed it. It would be simply passing from human passion to the love of God and finding a natural occupation for your soul: not to love at all would be a void that a heart like yours could not endure.' [26] It recalls the complaint of Catherine the Great, that her heart could not live an hour without love. And how vivid, further, is Saint-Évremond's reading of all Ninon's story in her eyes. 'I do not doubt that our friend found you with the same eyes that I used to see, in which I could always see the conquest of a lover, when they shone more than was their wont.' [27]

There is an even greater grace, candor, and intensity in Ninon's letters to her friend in England. There is the regret for the passage of youth, for the flight of years and the vanishing of charm and beauty. 'Ah!' she sighs, 'the days pass in idleness and ignorance, and these same days destroy us and rob us of all that we have loved.' [28] Memory has its charm, lasting friendship has its charm, but the things that are gone, what can bring them back? Yet if she has much to regret, she has nothing to repent. What a strange mistake it is of Matthew Arnold's by which, in lauding chastity, he quotes a well-known sentence of Ninon, 'If any one had proposed such a life to me, I should have hanged myself,' [29] as if she were referring to her past, when the context shows clearly that it is the present she condemns, in thinking of her past success and triumphs. No, there is little in the past that she would change, and her attitude is precisely that of her father, who regretted nothing about vanished pleasures except that they were so brief and that they could never be renewed.

Equally wise and serene with her acceptance of the departure of youth is Ninon's recognition of the coming of age. She is too clear-sighted not to appreciate all the drawbacks. The drooping of the

spirits, the stiffening of the muscles, the decay of
the faculties, and the loss of those we love — no one
understands these things better than she. But it is
the course of life, and must be met as such, with a
cheerful smile and a larger comprehension. There is
no trace in her of Sainte-Beuve's fierce appraisal,
'Ripen! Ripen! We never ripen. We rot in some
places, we harden in others, we ripen never.' [30]
There is not even the milder complaint of Shakespeare:

> And so from hour to hour we ripe and ripe,
> And then from hour to hour we rot and rot,
> And thereby hangs a tale.

It is rather the serene naturalism of Ninon's great
teacher, Montaigne, 'One of the chief obligations
I owe to fortune is that the course of my bodily
estate has brought each thing in its season: I have
seen the growth, the flowering, and the fruiting, and
now I see the decay: happily, because naturally.' [31]
Surely this is the attitude of the spirit which could
declare that 'the joy of a soul is the measure of its
force.'

And if there is a tranquil acceptance of life, so
there is also serene equanimity in the face of death.
There is no delusion. Ninon allowed the priests to
bustle and chatter about her, like the rest of the

world, but they did not impress her late any more
than they did early. The best she could find to say
of the future was that it would be pleasant to believe, with Madame de Chevreuse, that one might
spend it in converse with one's friends,[32] but when
she lay upon her death-bed, she is said to have
written these verses:

> Qu'un vain espoir ne vienne point s'offrir
>   Qui puisse ébranler mon courage.
> Je suis en âge de mourir,
>   Que ferais-je ici davantage?
>
> I put your consolations by,
>   And care not for the hopes you give:
> Since I am old enough to die,
>   Why should I longer wish to live? [33]

Still happily, because naturally.

So, in this wild and wayward woman, who flung
herself into life as a girl, fearless and independent,
and lived it out to the last grip of old age, just as
independent and just as fearless, I think we may
trace something of the splendid spiritual poise that
Matthew Arnold celebrated in the greatest of the
Attic dramatists,

> Whose even-balanced soul,
> From first youth tested even to extreme old age,
> Business could not make dull, nor passion wild,
> Who saw life steadily and saw it whole.[34]

DAUGHTERS OF EVE

But I prefer to associate with Ninon the untranslatable loveliness of the line which Sophocles himself puts into the mouth of Antigone,

οὔ τοι συνέχθειν ἀλλὰ συμφιλεῖν ἔφυν.
I was not born to hate, but born to love.[35]

No epitaph could be fitter for Ninon de Lenclos.

II
EVE AS DOVE AND SERPENT
MADAME DE MAINTENON

CHRONOLOGY

Françoise d'Aubigné.
Born, Niort, France, November 27, 1635.
In Martinique, 1645–1647.
Father died, 1647.
Married Scarron, 1652.
Took charge of Madame de Montespan's children by King, 1669.
Married King, 1684.
Saint-Cyr founded, 1686.
King died, 1715.
Died, April 15, 1719.

II
MADAME DE MAINTENON

I

THAT a poor girl who had kept geese in the fields should come to marry the greatest king in the world sounds like a fairy tale, and the story of Madame de Maintenon has much of dream quality about it. Yet the heroine does not give the impression of anything fairylike. She was just a creature of plain, cool common sense and enormously determined will, set upon getting the best that life had to give and getting it, yet all the time proclaiming and probably feeling the utter worthlessness of this life compared to another.

Françoise d'Aubigné was born in Niort, in 1635. She was the granddaughter of Agrippa d'Aubigné, a great Huguenot fighter and writer. Her father was a worthless scamp, who was often in prison, martyred her virtuous but narrow-minded mother, and died Governor of Martinique in 1647. After her return to France, Françoise was tossed about among different relatives and had a rude battle with poverty, even to the goose tending. For a time she was in a convent, and though she long stuck to her Protestantism, she at last succumbed. To escape dependence or religion, she married the paralytic poet Scarron and with him she lived for years in a wild set, but she kept a steady, cool head through all the wildness. After Scarron's death she was poor again, but she made powerful friends and fought her way up till King Louis XIV and Madame de Montespan induced her to assume the care of their illegitimate children. In this function she was magnificently devoted, and though the King did not take to her at first, she charmed him, as she did every one, till he made her Marquise de Maintenon, gave her a great estate, abandoned Madame de Montespan and all other loves for her, and finally beyond a doubt married her, in 1684, though no actual record of the marriage exists. For thirty years she was practically queen, though never publicly recognized. For thirty years she maintained her position with a tact, a patience, a dignity, an infinite resource, and an infinite weariness that no born queen ever surpassed. Then in 1715, when she was eighty years old, the King died, and her glory went out like a snuffed candle. The remaining four years of her life were passed in retirement in the Convent of Saint-Cyr, which she had established as a refuge for young girls who, like herself, were well born but poor, and to which she had turned in her later years with ever-increasing interest and devotion.

In this extraordinary and almost unparalleled career the fascinating thing is the study of the twisted tangle of motives, and vast as the material is, to untwist that tangle is so difficult that one is sometimes tempted to accept Madame de Maintenon's own remark, that she wished 'to remain an enigma to posterity.' [1]

It cannot be questioned that there was a steady purpose, or perhaps we should rather say, an instinct, to rise, to get ahead in the world, to get power and prominence and public consideration and esteem. Gleams of these things shine out with indubitable clearness in her own words. In middle life she speaks of herself as 'wholly leavened with glory and self-love.' [2] And looking back in old age, she paints the same passion as vividly as possible: 'I have never seen any one who was like me in that respect: I was sensitive to the praises of the King and I was just as sensitive to those of a laborer, and there is nothing that I should not have been capable of doing or suffering to get well spoken of.' [3]

The curious thing is that she steadily and persistently disclaims any ambition or desire whatever for position and power. And no doubt this is usual with all who seek the good things of the world, but with few is it so marked and so assertive as with Madame de Maintenon. People believe that she could not have got where she is, she says, without the utmost skillful management, and yet really she is candid and simple and quite incapable of any management whatever.[4] She does not admit herself to be fit for great station or equal to it any more than she is desirous of it, and she deprecates all attribution of greatness. As she puts it, in one of her admirable phrases, 'I am not great, I am only elevated.'[5] She subdues herself, she withdraws herself, she effaces herself, keeps in the background, as if she were a saint rather than a queen. Long, long before the termination of her career she writes to her dear friend the Archbishop of Paris: 'God has given me the grace to be insensible to the honors that surround me and to feel only the subjection and the constraint of them: pride in these matters has long been dead in me.'[6]

For not only was she indifferent to the glamor of high station and the splendors of the moving world, she professed to despise and hate them, even in the earlier days before her marriage with the King. In the height of her grandeur she bewails the emptiness of it: 'Don't you see that I am dying of grief and melancholy in the midst of a good fortune that could hardly have been imagined, and that only the aid of God keeps me from succumbing? I have been young and beautiful, and I was universally loved; when I was a little older, I passed years in the whirl of wit; I got the favor of the great. Yet I protest to you, my dear child, that all these varied conditions leave a horrible void, a disquiet, a lassitude, a longing to know something different, because none of them is adequate to satisfy us: there is no repose unless one gives oneself to God.' [7] So all through her long career, early and late, there is a continual outcry, or more properly murmur, for repose, tranquillity, escape, and peace.

And one naturally asks oneself, if she wanted these things, why she did not have them? During the years when she was most restless, up to the time of her marriage with the King, she could surely have retired, if she had wished, and even later, not being formally recognized, she might have secluded herself in Saint-Cyr or elsewhere, and let the King come to her. The answer she gives us, and no doubt gave herself, is duty and the call of God. These Montespan children of sin were her charge, to be cared for and saved, if she could save them.

Still more, as her influence with the King grew, she saw her duty to save him, to pull him out of his debaucheries and make him the savior of his people and a child of Heaven. Her confessor told her it was her duty, the wisest men in France told her so, and she saw it so herself; there can be no question but that she was perfectly sincere. Such passages as the following bring out the complication with fascinating clearness: 'I regard myself as an instrument in the hands of God to do good, and all the credit that He permits me to have must be employed in serving Him, in helping everybody I can help, and in bringing all these princes into harmony.'[8]

For, under all the duty and all the religion, you feel an immense and constant contentment in her station and her power over 'all these princes' and an almost avid enjoyment of it. Who can blame her? She had begun life in poverty and misery, tossed about from one relative to another, a burden to all, and patronized and pitied by all alike. Now she was at the top. Kings bowed down to her. Rival ladies flattered her. Ministers and generals deferred to her opinion. It seemed at times as if the world could not go on if she withdrew her consent. She felt the hollowness of it all. She doubted very much if she could save herself in such a whirl-pool of wickedness, let alone any one else. She often and often wished she were well out of it. Yet if she had been out of it, she would have perished with longing to be back, and she enjoyed it enormously: what woman would not? or what man either?

II

We shall get somewhat more light on all these complications when we look a little more closely into the general elements of Madame de Maintenon's character, though it may also seem as if the complications increased.

She had a clear, logical, vigorous intellect. There was no very substantial education behind it, nor was she ever an eager reader, though she had a gift of absorbing what she wanted. Her intelligence had its marked limits. She cared nothing for abstract thinking, nothing for history or philosophy, and this limitation imperiled the value of her larger influence. But she had magnificent common sense, as Louis well knew when he called her 'votre solidité.' Perhaps the two words that occur most frequently with her are reason — reasonableness — and simplicity. She would have liked to combine

the wisdom of the serpent with the simplicity of
the dove. 'You know that my mania is to make
people hear reason,' she cries.[9] Control of passion
and whim and impulse by a calm and reasoned
judgment was her theory, her effort, and her practice. We may sometimes be tempted to say with
Boissier, 'she reasoned all her life, and as the excess
of a quality becomes a defect, we end by thinking
her a little too reasonable.' [10] But for good or evil,
it is her distinguishing characteristic, and she had a
passion for imparting it to her friends. Like many
people with good minds, she was much less interested in using her intelligence for itself than in
training others to use theirs. That is, she was what
would now be called an educator, and educating
was her passion, early and late.

If she cared little for the abstract aspects of intellectual life, she cared even less for what may be
called the ornaments of it. Art meant nothing to
her. To painting she was quite indifferent, to
music almost as much so. Ardently as she longs for
retirement, she never turns to nature. She wanted
a great country place, and she got it, but she wanted
the sense of proprietorship, not the charm of out of
doors, and in this respect, as in so many others, she
is strikingly contrasted with her charming con-

temporary, Madame de Sévigné. Even literature was unimportant. She had great poets in her circle, notably Racine, who wrote 'Esther' and 'Athalie' for her protégées to act. But this bred passion and worldliness and she regretted it. She wrote to Racine: 'Our little girls acted "Andromaque" yesterday: they did it so well that they will never do it again or any of your pieces.' [11] And she disposes of the whole business of literary art and mental activity generally in one swift, fierce sentence: 'Do not seek what pleases the intelligence: it is nothing but vanity.' [12]

With these views, it would not be likely that she would be much tempted by authorship. Nor was she, though she occasionally wrote verses, like almost everybody else in that day. But she did write letters, enormously. Many of them have perished. She herself destroyed those written to the King and others. Yet a great quantity remain, and her first biographer, La Beaumelle, saw fit to forge a large number, thus causing annoyance and confusion to historians and biographers ever since.

Madame de Maintenon was proud of her letters and had reason to be. They have not the charm of Madame de Sévigné's, because the writer had not. But all critics praise them as the perfection of seventeenth-century French, and for us they have the value of an extraordinary richness of self-revelation. One not inconsiderable element of this is the singular adaptability to different correspondents. This multiple and complicated spirit, who prided herself on being sincere and unquestionably was so, could write to a saint with all the fine flavor of saintliness, and to a sinner, not indeed with a flavor of sin, but at least with a suggestion that human weakness was not alien to her. To her friends of the cloister she speaks with an encloistered purity, and to the man of the world she writes as a fully developed woman of the world might.

For, though her intelligence may not have been alert in regions of speculation or ornament, it was immensely active, acute, and penetrating in what concerned the daily life that crowded and flowed about her. Saint-Simon says, and indeed she herself says, that she was often duped, but if so, it was when she was willing to be. For her comprehension of life and character in general seems to have been singularly keen. And, alas! the result of such long experience of the world was too often disillusion, not to say bitterness. 'I see passions of all sorts,' she says, 'treasons, baseness, limitless ambition;

on one side horrible desire, on the other people with rage at heart, who seek only to destroy each other; in sum, a thousand evil devices, and often for objects that are utterly trifling.' [13]

Yet it was a principle with her not to allow the bitterness to appear. Gentleness, kindness, above all, reticence were absolutely necessary to success in life, and any cynicism that developed in her heart was not permitted to affect her tongue. But whether, after all, the motive of such reticence was kindness or caution we are left somewhat in doubt, as with so many of the aspects of her spirit.

For she applied the same keen vision to herself that she had ready for others, and she analyzes her own defects with surprising acuteness and merciless severity. Take religion. She loves it, she longs for it. Yet all the time she doubts whether her love and longing are rooted in a real inclination of heart: 'A thousand times I have wanted to enter the religious life, and the fear of being sorry has made me slight impulses that a thousand persons would have taken for a serious call.' [14] Again, she plans a spiritual retreat, and a sudden whiff of discouragement makes her fear that 'the devotion that I look for is merely the same instinct of tidiness that I feel in arranging the furniture at Maintenon.' [15]

And it is curious to see how, in this analysis of faults, she manages, as we so often do, deftly to turn faults into virtues. Indeed, it must be admitted that she has a rather flagrant gift of self-commendation. This is partly explained by the never-failing teacher's instinct to set an example and to edify. Yet the reiteration of it, even though graceful and tactful, is a little wearying. 'God gives me grace never to vex anybody.' [16] It may be true, but the compliment would have more savor if it came from some other source.

If she had a vast knowledge of life, there was every reason why she should have, for few persons have seen more of it. And her position was peculiar in that she had seen the darker lining before she was confronted with the glittering outside. Queens are generally flattered and courted from their birth; but she had been kicked and buffeted and pitied, before she was adored, and it made her somewhat sceptical about the adoration. She came into contact with all sorts of human beings by hundreds, but there is no sign that she greatly enjoyed it.

Even in the early Scarron days she was remote and dignified. She could be animated and eager on occasion, and she was sought and loved. Still there was always the sense that she was a little above and apart. The diversions that excite ordinary men and women did not appeal to her. She played cards, and when she was old and solitary a game of tric-trac was better than her thoughts, but she detested gambling, did not like to lose her own money or win others', and in general amusements were a a weariness.

So with conversation. She was an adept at it. She had wit, and variety, and color, and gayety, when she chose. Madame de Sévigné, who lived intimately with her in the earlier days, says that her company was delicious.[17] The most curious story bearing on this point is that of the confessor who, appreciating the brilliancy of her speech, urged her to control it and practice silence for the good of her soul. Her friends could not understand her dumbness and bewailed it, until she explained the cause, adding that it had almost disgusted her with religion for good. But as life went on, she grew more and more mistrustful of the tongue, and she urged her protégées to bridle it, to mortify it, to forget it: 'Renouncing all sensibility to clever-ness, the desire to possess it, to exhibit it, to find it in others, discarding the vanity of eloquence, the curiosity to hear those who speak well because they divert our intelligence and stimulate a taste which we should mortify far rather than excite it or even cherish it.' [18]

But, however she may have disapproved of conversation or any other social agency, there is no doubt that she availed herself of them with exquisite skill, to win, to conquer, and to retain admiration and affection. She had sympathy, she had understanding, she had tact, could see what people wanted and needed, and she was ready to efface herself in the effort to give it to them. As to these qualities and her success in the use of them there is abundant and universal testimony, but I do not know that it would be possible to find any keener analysis of this success than her own, though again it comes somewhat strangely from that source, and the strangeness is not diminished by her reflective comment that her care for others did not spring from affection so much as from a desire to conciliate: 'I had an excellent disposition, a kindly heart, in other words, I was really what is called a good child, so that everybody loved me and that even the men and maid servants of my aunt, with whom I then lived, were charmed with me, and simply because I thought only of making myself agreeable to them. When I was a little older, I lived in convents: you know how much I was beloved by my mistresses and my companions; I have often told you that they were delighted to have me and always for the same reason: it was because I did them services, and I thought of nothing but obliging them and doing things for them from morning till night.' [19] The statement may be somewhat astonishing, but the fact seems indisputable.

How far her charm came from merely physical attraction it is difficult to say. In the portraits, mostly dating from later life, she seems to us dignified and imposing, but somewhat stiff and heavy, of feature and of figure, perhaps in part owing to the stiffness of garb. But contemporaries found a beauty of expression which we can hardly define. As one of them describes it: 'The sound of her voice was most agreeable, her tone was affectionate and tender. She had an open and cordial brow, the natural gestures of a beautiful hand, eyes of fire, a flexible figure, so sensitive and so well formed that she eclipsed the loveliest ladies of the Court.... At first sight she was imposing and as it were somewhat veiled with severity; but the smile and the voice broke through the cloud.' [20]

At any rate, whatever the nature or the analysis of the charm, it is admitted by every one, even by

those, like Saint-Simon and the German Duchess of
Orleans, who detested her most.

III

It was the charm that made her queen and kept
her queen for thirty years. And it is most curiously
interesting to watch, to trace, to divine the gradual
steady growth of her position and influence. The
influence involved Madame de Montespan first,
and it was not qualified by jealousy so long as the
King seemed indifferent or almost averse. But as
he discovered the stranger's good qualities and
turned to her for comfort and guidance, Madame
de Montespan became irritated, and there were
violent scenes between the two; yet Madame de
Maintenon quietly held her own, and she fore-
stalled criticism of treachery to her former bene-
factress by alleging to her confessor, to others in
later life, and no doubt sincerely to herself, that she
was doing her best to save the King's soul and that
of Madame de Montespan also.

When the royal children outgrew her, she accepted a court position, and always her influence
quietly increased. The King turned to her more
and more, but she resisted anything of an illicit
nature in the spirit of her own maxim, which ir-

ritated Sainte-Beuve so much for its cold-blooded, if profoundly practical wisdom: 'There is nothing so clever as not to be in the wrong and to bear oneself irreproachably at all times and with all sorts of people.' [21] We seem to be listening to Benjamin Franklin, and there was undeniably a certain spiritual affinity between the two.

With infinite tact Madame de Maintenon made herself indispensable to the Queen as well as to the King, for there was an insignificant Queen, though one might never suspect it. The wise lady drew King and Queen together as they had not been for years, and the Queen was duly grateful. Then, by a strange freak of fortune, which could not have been foreseen, the Queen was removed from this world. Madame de Maintenon spoke of leaving the Court at once, but she did not, and after a period of debate and hesitation, Louis, although he was some years younger than she, offered her his hand and crown, and she became queen in all but the name. Perhaps, as Saint-Simon insists, she would have liked the name also, but even he is forced to admit that, with extraordinary wisdom and self-control, she recognized that this was impossible and contented herself with being the first lady and being universally known as such.

Did she use her power for her own purposes?
Apparently with the utmost moderation. She
helped her relatives where she could, but again and
again she points out to them that she can do only
so much and that she will not imperil her position
to bring them a doubtful benefit. For herself she
asked comparatively little. She did indeed have
her title and estate and a pension to maintain them.
But her habits of living and appearing were always
simple and she kept them so, even effacing herself
almost obtrusively. There was no trace of greed
about her, or of grasping for gain any more than for
glory.

Did she use her power for the good of France?
Her enemies say she was a baneful influence, turning the King to narrow views and measures that
were disastrous. Her admirers insist that she did
not meddle at all, that the King would not have
listened to her and that she did not wish him to.
The truth is probably, as usual, between the two
views. Her limitation of knowledge and of broad intellectual interest, which I have already indicated,
prevented her from taking any such hold of world
affairs as Elizabeth of England had or Catherine of
Russia. It seems certain that the bitterest charge
of her enemies, that she urged the Revocation of

the Edict of Nantes, which drove the best of the Huguenots out of the country, is quite unfounded. But on the other hand it is impossible not to believe that, she being what she was, and Louis being what he was, and their relation being what it was, her influence was not constant and very great.

It is true that it was subtle and obscure. She took the utmost pains to keep herself in the background, and repeated and reiterated that she had no concern with public affairs whatever. This appears so often that many of her apologists insist upon her being taken at her word. But it requires very little knowledge of the world to give such assertions their true value and no more. One of her humble, conventual friends artlessly unveils the secret in a brief sentence: 'It never appeared that she had the slightest desire to be declared queen.... It was her humble and hidden life that made her power.' [22] And Saint-Simon quotes from her own nephew an admirable account of the roundabout way in which she had to work to get the King to attend to her wishes: 'In order to succeed in what she wished, she was very careful to have it proposed by some one else, simply made it her business to support the suggestion, when the King consulted her about it, as he invariably did with everything, and by this device, which kept from the King the knowledge of what she was aiming at, she never failed to obtain it.' [23]

Yet, however delicate the method of management was, or precisely because it was delicate, the management was solid, lasting, and effective. Almost any wife will understand the nature of it. Are there not millions of American wives, apparently considerate and deferential, keeping suavely and deftly within their own province, yet at the same time having their little, dainty fingers on every pulse of their world? So it was with Madame de Maintenon. And King Louis the Fourteenth was just an ordinary husband. He liked his royal, masculine authority. He liked to assert it and maintain it. No one should teach him or show him what to do. The inferiority complex which Mr. Huddleston has analyzed in him so skillfully made him touchy and sensitive as to any attempt to control him. Yet a quiet word in the right place at the right moment, the light touch of a suggesting hand would do wonders. And again and again Madame de Maintenon's correspondence gives flashes of insight into what she did and how she did it. To suggest, to indicate, to imply was enough. Are there not volumes in her brief sentence, 'Sometimes you have to deceive the King for his own good'? [24] And how much careful, patient study shows in remarks like the following: 'For some time the King has kept a silence which I mistrust very much.... You know his anger is not in the first outburst and it grows as he thinks things over and dwells upon them.' [25]

As it is obvious that she possessed a wifely and so a queenly power, it is equally obvious that she enjoyed it. She liked to be present at the councils of state, and she generally was, oh, unobtrusively, sitting in a far corner with her embroidery, but she was there, and now and then a question was referred to her, always against her modest protest, and the questions could be more freely talked over afterwards. She liked to discuss with Madame des Ursins the welfare of Spain, where the King was the French King's grandson. She liked to have the ministers and the generals visit her obsequiously, and talk over their plans, and get her suggestions and advice. Above all, she liked princes and nobles and priests and great ones to bow down to her and flatter her, her whom in the old days even little ones had trampled on. The heir to the throne and his son and their wives caressed her and petted her and looked up to her, and of course she liked it.

And there was the great scene of triumph when that rude old Duchess of Orleans, who hated her, was humbled so completely. The Duchess swept down upon her with abuse and complaint. Madame de Maintenon quietly produced a letter, written home to the Duchess's relatives in Germany, scolding about everybody, from the King down, and the old woman wept and trembled and apologized, with abject dread. And Madame de Maintenon was magnanimous and gentle and forgiving, with what a wave of triumph in her heart, and how the old woman must have hated her then!

Which was all very well, but there were terrible drawbacks. There was a lot of this hatred and jealousy and spite, which no gentleness or tact could overcome. And the King himself was difficult. He really loved his wife, but he was accustomed to having his own way, and he had little consideration. He taxed her strength and her patience and her good-nature. He had no regard for fatigue or discomfort, when they were not his own. He wanted fresh air, and Madame de Maintenon hated the cold. He wanted attention when she was tired, when she was hungry, when she was ill. The court routine was infinitely complicated and infinitely wearisome. As she puts it in one splendidly effective phrase: 'You can't arrange your room as you like, when the King comes to it every day, and you have to perish in symmetry.' [26] As she grew older, the weariness overcame her more and more. On the whole, she was remarkably of a piece all her life, the same woman at thirty and at eighty; but age did tell, and with the progress of years, she was sometimes oppressed with the hollowness, the futility of it all. Could there be a more tragic picture of the decay of greatness than her description of herself to Madame des Ursins in the later years? 'If you could see me, you would agree that I do well to keep myself hid: my eyesight is poor, my hearing is worse; nobody can hear me, for my speech has gone with my teeth; my memory goes astray, I no longer recall proper names, I mix up different periods; and misfortune and age together make me weep like all the other old women you have known.' [27]

So, as the glory of the world fell away from her, she turned more and more to her retirement at Saint-Cyr, the group of teachers and pupils who had been absorbing her affection and attention for so many years. At a very early period she had persuaded the King to let her found an educational institution for poor girls of good families, and with time the establishment, moving into ampler quarters, had become a very important affair. At first she had wished it to be secular in organization, but as she went on and found how great and troublesome the worldly temptations and surroundings were, she finally succeeded in putting the school on a conventual basis, and as such it continued for many years after her death.

Here, as everywhere, she reveled in management. She advised and suggested and directed, and looked after every detail with loving, persistent care. Above all, she had the chance to let loose all her educational proclivities. She not only dictated what the girls should study, but what they should read, and what they should wear, and what they should eat, and, as far as possible, what they should think. The minuteness, the constancy of her control is astonishing. And every now and again it comes over me, what did the teachers and the girls really feel about it? We have their formal expressions of love and gratitude. Was their inner judgment the same? Did they resent such perpetual dictation? Or were her tact and sympathy sufficient to make her beloved through it all? In any event one sees everywhere the devoted woman, always intent on managing the affairs of those she loves.

IV

And one asks oneself how far she really was a woman, in her tastes and habits and interests? For instance, did she care for those household affairs, which, in former days at any rate, were supposed to be a woman's main concern? Apparently she did. When she went to Saint-Cyr, she could step right into the kitchen, put on an apron, and cook. If any one objected that she would smell of onions in the parlor, she laughed, and said, 'That's all right: they will not believe it is I.' She was a good housewife, careful and orderly in everything. Above all, as in other larger matters, she was ready to give advice, as to sewing, as to cooking, as to the most important business of domestic expenses. And she hands her needy brother a detailed schedule of just what his table ought to cost. She sums up these feminine matters with a delicate touch when she describes herself as 'moi qui suis très-femmelette.' [28]

So with servants. Necessarily she had a large staff of them, and she emphasizes the importance of being mistress and avoiding undue familiarity. But also she is profoundly and broadly human. Servants are men and women and should be treated as such: you must not expect perfection for it does not exist: 'one should use people according to their gifts and consider that none are perfect.' [29] Consequently, her servants were quiet, swift, and efficient, as even the hostile Saint-Simon grudgingly concedes. And, if one may believe her own testimony, they were devotedly attached to her. Of one lackey, for whom she was trying to find a place, she says: 'He has served me with an affection that I can never recompense.' [30] And her maid Nanon clung to her for years, with persistent and unfaltering fidelity.

As to dress, she was a woman also. She was interested in the little details, and writes with minute care about the change of fashion and the choice of stuffs. But for herself she dressed with a severe simplicity, almost to the point of making a parade of it. Here again we have those delightful touches of self-commendation, which are so simple, so earnest, and so revealing: 'People were never tired of wondering how a young girl, in the full tide of society, had the courage to keep up so modest a fashion of dressing.' [31] And once more Saint-Simon bears her out. Yet the flutter of feminine coquetry creeps and peeps under all the modesty, as in the charming anecdote of the confessor who complained of her elegance. But, she protested, see how simple my dress is! And he shook his head: 'When you go down on your knees, a flood of stuffs falls about you at my feet, and it is all so graceful that somehow it strikes me as too attractive.' [32] Still and always the woman's mystery and mastery of sex!

In the matter of health, again, Madame de Maintenon is interesting to follow. When you consider the busy life she lived, you would think she must have been robust; yet she complains that she has been always unhealthy, though, as she puts it, 'her caducity is vigorous.' [33] She has very little confidence in doctors and avoids them when possible, yet she is perfectly ready to counsel others as to all sorts of regimens and remedies: perhaps her vast experience, direct and indirect, made this not altogether unjustifiable.

As to money she is the same thrifty, careful housewife that she is in other matters. Her large establishment required a fairly abundant supply, and she always had it. But she did not spend on herself, did not care to, and she was true to her own saying, 'The longer I live, the more I grow in the opinion that it is useless to pile up wealth.' [34] What she most wanted money for was to give away. She had been poor herself, she knew what poverty was, and so far as she had means, she meant to get rid of all the suffering she could. Yet even here she did not propose to be duped, and the calm, clear judgment was always at work. She would help only those who were worth helping, and she took pains to find who the worthy were: 'I am determined to aid those who aid themselves, and to let the good-for-nothing suffer.' [35]

As to her human relations, her affections, her friendships, the question is more complicated. She herself insists that she was profoundly affectionate and deeply and permanently loyal. She had a sensitive and loving heart, and craved response from others. In a sense she appears to have got it; yet once more, I would give a good deal to know what her friends really thought of her in this connection. There is no doubt about her enemies, and Saint-Simon makes it his most severe charge against her that she was quite unreliable, would adore you to-day and forget you to-morrow. No doubt he exaggerates. Yet she did get rid of those whom she had loved in a rather unfortunate fashion. Her conduct to Madame de Montespan is hard to forgive. Madame de Brinon, the head of Saint-Cyr, she caressed and flattered, and then turned her out, probably for good reasons; but still ——. Fénelon she worshiped, and abandoned, and the Cardinal de Noailles in the same way. It is a curious thing that she managed to keep friendly relations with them all, but the break was there. Perhaps there is profound truth in Sainte-Beuve's remark that she 'busied herself with people without loving them.' [36]

What she really and undeniably did love was children. Of course she liked to care for them and educate them, with her pedagogic disposition; but there was more to it than that. She clung to them and they to her, with a tenderness that peeps out everywhere. Her advice to one of her teachers goes straight to the heart: 'Begin by making them love you, otherwise you will never succeed.' [37] How moving is her outcry about one of her royal charges, the Duke of Maine: 'Nothing can be more foolish than to pour out this excess of love on a child who is not my own.' [38] One sees in a flash what it would have meant to have had a real husband and a flock of children. Perhaps she would have found it better than a court and a king.

If she had no children of her own, she had relatives, and she gave them almost as much care and attention as if they were her children. She watched over her nephews and nieces and cousins, advised them, provided for them, and was so interested in

their spiritual welfare that she even kidnapped a
niece to make sure of getting her into the true
church. If she approved of this for Huguenot
families generally, why not practice it in her own?
This niece, Madame de Caylus, a charming if somewhat erratic person, was almost like a daughter.
But the most profitable element of Madame de
Maintenon's family affection for us is the long
series of letters to her brother, D'Aubigné. He was
a wild fellow, like his father, and his sister had a
hard struggle to keep him upright in the world.
She got positions for him, she got money for him,
and above all, after much nice financial calculation,
she got a wealthy wife for him. And then she added
the most intimate domestic counsel, in a fashion
which seems somewhat odd when she herself admits that she had never been really married.

For what interests us most in this varied and
complicated tangle of affections is the question of
Madame de Maintenon's attitude towards the
supreme affection, that of sex. Apparently it
meant little to her. She herself tells us that 'thanks
to the goodness of God, I have no passions, that is
to say, I love no one to the point of being willing to
do anything that God would not approve.' [39] And
one of the ladies from whom she tried to wean the

King remarked to her indignantly: 'Madam, you talk of changing a passion as you would talk of changing a shirt.' [40]

It is true that her enemies piled up scandal about the gay years in the Scarron circle. Madame Scarron was an intimate friend of Ninon de Lenclos, the great lover of the time, and the association was dubious to say the least. Ninon, who was always a truth-teller, offers some evidence which it is hard to discount. Yet it seems possible, if not probable, that a strong foundation of religious principle, powerfully aided by a cold temperament and especially a determination to keep credit with the world, sustained Madame de Maintenon's virtue all through. As Jules Lemaître says, it is somewhat hard to believe that she came to King Louis at fifty quite intact, and one always remembers the remark of the witty lady, whose husband was loudly proclaiming Madame de Maintenon's innocence, 'My dear sir, how do you manage to be so sure of these things?' Yet her character and her history in general inspire a moderate amount of confidence.

At any rate, from her vast contact with life she had extracted a disgust for marriage and horror of men. She cannot warn her pupils often enough against those scheming creatures who make it their first object to caress and to betray. And of marriage the best she finds to say is, that it is 'a state that causes the misery of three quarters of the human race.' [41]

Which immediately makes one curious about her relation to her own royal husband. As to his feeling there can be no doubt. By some magic that we can hardly understand he adored her for the whole thirty years and came to depend upon her more and more. There is a touching veracity and force in her own account of his dying words and her comment on them: 'He himself said to me when he was dying: "I have not made you happy," at the same time assuring me that I was all he regretted and that he had loved me always.... It is true that he loved me, and more than he loved any one else; but he loved me only so much as he was capable of loving; for men, when passion does not carry them away, are not very tender in their affection.' [42] And the further account of that death scene reveals with a wonderful delicacy and clarity some of the intertwining strands of feeling in both of them, as there is nothing for revelation like these great crises of life. When the end drew near, the King began to mourn because she was not sufficiently provided for. 'What will become of you?' he said. And she answered passionately: 'What is all that now? Your own future is the only thing that counts.' And then, with the sober second thought so characteristic of her, she murmured that perhaps he might say a word to the Duke of Orleans, who would be regent, to see that she was properly looked after.

Which suggests the more subtle and difficult problem of her feeling for him. Whether she had much has been questioned on the ground of her having fled to Saint-Cyr before the breath was actually out of his body. But she had been told that he would never know her again, and she had herself to take care of. When he did recover consciousness, she hurried back.

Still, it can hardly be maintained that she was passionately fond of him. A sort of maternal tenderness, a long regard she had. And further, there was that old puzzle, which none of us can ever quite solve, the relation of affection and need. Her power, her fortune, her happiness, so far as she had any, her life, depended on his: how was she to tell what was need and what was love? How are any of us to tell? When he was taken from her, her world went to pieces. It had already gone to pieces in a manner, by the succession of terrific tragedies that

carried off first the King's son, and then his grandson and granddaughter-in-law, on whom Madame
de Maintenon had built all her hopes. Then Louis
himself died, and what was there left? Unless a
shadowy comfort in the future power of the Duke
of Maine, which also was brought to nothing by
the establishment of the Orleans supremacy. After
this, Madame de Maintenon's old age in the solitude of Saint-Cyr was total eclipse. She bore it all
with courage, with patience, with a sort of dreary
serenity of grief, finding her greatest comfort in
doing good to those about her, so far as she could.
But the King, and the husband, and the glory, and
the power were all gone together, and it would have
taken a shrewder wit than even hers to distinguish
one from the others.

v

It was fortunate that through this arid waste of
desolation she had God to comfort her, as she always had. In her Protestant youth she had established a personal relation with the Deity, and she
maintained it through all her change of creed,
reading the Bible, especially the New Testament,
especially Saint Paul, more perhaps than is usual
with Catholics. Through all the misery and gayety

of her earlier years, through the vicissitudes of her middle life, through the wit of Scarron and the wiles of Montespan and the worldly wisdom of King Louis, she thought of God, she talked God, and as was her nature, she preached God to others.

Her enemies called it hypocrisy, but there is no doubt whatever that she was absolutely sincere. She herself insists, probably with justice, that she had a simple, direct, frank nature, to which dissimulation was abhorrent. The hard ways of the world, of which she had traveled so many, had forced her to be reserved, to keep her thoughts to herself, even at times to deceive others for their good. But she hated it, and would have preferred to say right out what she thought about everything. When she spoke of God, she meant what she said. Rarely has anything finer been written about sincerity than her simple words: 'Frankness does not consist in saying a great deal, but in saying everything, and this everything is soon said when one is sincere, because there is no need of a great flourish and because one does not need many words to open the heart.' [43]

But if her religion was genuine, it was also perfectly practical, redolent of the common sense which characterized her in all things, and always shy of the fantastic or extreme. As she puts it, 'I never cease attacking this fancy for revelations, for ecstasies, in a word, for extraordinary ways of getting at simple ends.' [44] In this connection it is most interesting to study her dealings with the great Fénelon. At first his earnestness, his purity, his elevation charmed her: she thought of making him her spiritual director. But when he became involved with Madame Guyon and mysticism and Quietism, when she saw that these notions were working havoc among her flock at Saint-Cyr and that the King distinctly disapproved, she shifted at once. Firm earth was good enough for her. She left these airy regions to others, and Fénelon and Madame Guyon were laid aside. So with the Archbishop, afterwards Cardinal, de Noailles. For a long time she turned to him for everything, but when he clung to the heresies of Jansenism, against the decrees of the Church and the wishes of the King, she abandoned him, with regret, but with swift and sharp decision.

For an unfailing reasonableness governed her spiritual concerns as well as her worldly. The ways of rapture, of high-wrought, supra-mundane forgetfulness were not for her. To be sure, her persistent reading of the 'Imitation,' of Saint Francis of Sales, of Fénelon sometimes gives her letters a touch of their unearthly tone, but it was not natural to her. Her religion has at all times a bread and butter flavor, and what interested her supremely was to save herself, to save others, especially the King, to save everybody.

In short, her instinct for managing the world was just as marked in religion as in everything, indeed even more marked. There may be some question as to how much she interfered in the politics of this world: they did not interest her. There can be no doubt whatever as to the part she took in the politics of another. She had Fénelon made Archbishop of Cambrai — and regretted it. She had Noailles made Archbishop of Paris — and regretted it. But such things did not discourage her, and she advised the King, in her quiet, thoughtful, cautious way, as long as he lived. If it seemed to her that too many bishops were hanging about the Court, instead of attending to their dioceses, she said a word in the royal ear — and there was a speedy exodus of bishops.

And if she enjoyed general religious politics, she enjoyed even more the detail of religious management with individuals. To look over the vast mass of letters that she wrote to her various teachers and pupils gives an extraordinary sense of intimate personal direction, much as one gets it from the correspondence of Fénelon or Saint Francis. She guides the spiritual as well as the temporal affairs of all these girls, whom she evidently loves, with a closeness of personal touch that is almost incomprehensible in a woman who was so desperately entangled in all the bustle of the great world. She chides, she cheers, she warns, she encourages, she instructs, with tireless patience and a flow of words that seems absolutely inexhaustible. And the tone is so sincere and so affectionate that it does not weary. Yet, as always, one does wonder how her correspondents took it. Were they responsive and grateful? Or did they occasionally rebel against the long sermoning of a tedious old woman? If they did, they had to keep it to themselves.

At least it must be remembered that she managed her own soul with the same discretion, the same reasonableness that she applied to others. Yet perhaps it is on this very account that she attracts us so little. For the lack of attraction is undeniable. We admit her virtue, we admire her achievements, we recognize the charm that she must have had. Only somehow the charm has evaporated with the passage of years. And always

one compares her with Madame de Sévigné, so
fresh, so spontaneous, so human, so budding and
gurgling with constant gayety and instinctive joy.
After three hundred years you can read Madame
de Sévigné's letters and fall in love with her. But
no matter how much you read Madame de Maintenon, no man, not even a king, could fall in love
with her now. Yet a king did once, and she had the
world at her feet, and found it vanity, which perhaps is just the reason why she gets our respect and
not our love.

III
EVE AND ALMIGHTY GOD
MADAME GUYON

CHRONOLOGY

Jeanne Marie Bouvières de La Mothe
Born, Montargis, France, April 13, 1648.
Married M. Guyon, March 21, 1664.
Husband died, July 21, 1676.
Went to Switzerland, July, 1681.
Returned to Paris, July, 1686.
Wrote Autobiography mainly in 1688.
First imprisoned, January 29, 1688.
Met Fénelon, 1688, or 1689.
Imprisoned in Bastille, 1698.
Finally released, 1702.
Died, Blois, June 9, 1717.

III
MADAME GUYON

I

IT is the charm of the psychographer's business that he can turn from one type of character to another that is different, even entirely contrasted, and enter with all the sympathy and understanding he possesses into the profound humanity of both. It is hard to imagine more violent opposites than Ninon de Lenclos, the child of this world, and Madame Guyon, the child of the next, with Madame de Maintenon as a sort of mean term between; yet all three surely have their places in a study of the Daughters of Eve.

Jeanne Marie Bouvières de La Mothe Guyon was born at Montargis, France, April 13, 1648. Her birth, according to her own account, was attended by some of the extraordinary circumstances which her vast autobiographic narrative connects with almost every incident of her life. She was delicate and ailing from childhood, and her temperament and early training would seem to suggest that she might have been comfortably and permanently disposed of in a convent. Her parents thought otherwise and finally got her married, in

1664, to a man of wealth and distinguished family. She lived with him twelve years and bore five children, but it appears that her married life was not very agreeable to herself or to others, and after her husband's death she turned more and more to religion. She provided for her children as best she could and then emigrated to Switzerland and took a leading part in various religious communities, coming deeply under the influence of a certain Père La Combe, who was destined to have a very deep effect upon her life. After doing a good deal of good and a good deal of harm in Switzerland, she returned to Paris, gained a prominent position there among notable people, for instance, Madame de Maintenon, and Fénelon, Archbishop of Cambrai, one of the subtlest minds and noblest souls of his time. But her novel ideas and teachings aroused the enmity of the conservatives, led by Bossuet. They probed and criticized her doctrine, attacked her morals, condemned her books, and put her in various places of confinement, finally for three years in the Bastille. After she was released, she was obliged to live in seclusion till her death in 1717, but she retained her religious enthusiasm till the end and also the love and admiration of the small group of friends who clung to her.

Before analyzing Madame Guyon's religious experience, which was the essential part of her life, it is necessary to consider her dealings with the practical world, so indispensable to all of us, however much we may dislike it. It does not appear that in her youth she got much satisfaction out of her family: eager and enthusiastic idealists rarely do. She herself says: 'I lived in the midst of trials from my childhood, either from sickness or from persecution.' [1] Probably the persecution was largely imaginary, possibly the sickness also; but they were deadly real to her.

With her father she seems to have had a certain amount of sympathy. But she saw comparatively little of him and he died when she was quite young. The daughter struggles heroically to be just to her mother, to indicate her good qualities and good intentions. Notably it was from her mother that she learned the wide beneficence that, according to her own account, was so prominent in both of them. But they did not get on together. Perhaps in some respects they were too much alike. Jeanne insists that her brother was preferred to herself and that his illnesses were tended and remedied much more considerately than hers. [2] Possibly on this account her brothers and sisters did not mean much to her, except the one elder sister who was in a religious community and did all she could to foster the mystical inclinations of her junior.

Nor does it appear that Madame Guyon's matrimonial record is much more satisfactory than the domestic. She had a huge capacity for loving, but at an early stage most of it was turned over to God and certainly very little of it went to her husband. In her childhood she read novels [3] and there is a shadowy glimpse of one candidate who might have been a real lover. The actual husband had no serious faults. Madame Guyon herself freely admits his virtues and also his fundamental affection for her. But her devotion bored him. He tried to divert it, to check it, to discourage it, to forbid it. When he failed, he grew irritable and irritated, and his temper reacted on her. Here again she endeavors to do justice and admits her own faults and failures with considerable frankness, at the same time, like most autobiographers, managing, half unconsciously, to insinuate a delicate interweaving of excellences with the defects.

Then in the background there was always the mother-in-law. Madame Guyon was not a person ever to have been happy in such a relationship, and here the friction was apparently constant. The mother-in-law advised, dictated, perhaps made herself indispensably useful in practical matters, and what was worst of all, her son turned to her habitually instead of to his wife. You cannot make a much more effective summing up than Madame Guyon's own when she says: 'My condition in marriage was rather that of a slave than that of a free woman.' 4 Yet with it all, as I have said, the capacity for love was there, and you feel that the woman might have been adored and adoring. You feel it in such tender touches as her charming phrase: 'Let us love without reasoning about it, and we shall find ourselves filled with love before others have found out the reasons that lead to loving.' 5 Only, early and late her profound and passionate soul was all turned in another direction from the domestic hearth.

Thus, she does not seem to have given much more of herself even to her children than to her parents or to her husband. She was a faithful and a dutiful mother. She cared for the children's education, she tended their ailments, she provided for their future, and perhaps she enjoyed them as much as she enjoyed anything earthly. The deaths, especially that of her little son, afflicted her deeply. Yet somehow it all seems remote from her real spirit. One daughter showed strong religious tendencies. Her mother was delighted and carried the child with her into Switzerland. There she cared for her physically and spiritually. Yet her comment, when the daughter was finally married, is immensely characteristic: 'As soon as her marriage gave her to another, I felt myself cut off from all that regarded her external life, with no further possibility of taking any part in it.' [6] Even more characteristic is her feeling that, when her children are ill or suffer in any way, it is a special visitation of Providence intended for trial and discipline to *her*. In other words, she constantly betrays the overwhelming preoccupation with self which so often appears in those whose chief desire is to get rid of it.

Again, this exaggeration of her own importance and the part she plays appears in her relations with those who served her. She has, as in so many other things, just and delicate observations as to the general bearing in such a relation. 'There should be firmness and charity, but little familiarity with servants.' [7] But when it comes to particular cases, the distortion will intrude. For instance, in her married life there is one favorite maid in her husband's family who is a perpetual trial to the mistress, no doubt placed there for that special purpose,

and her spite and ill-nature are elevated to heights
of supernatural malignity, afterwards to be disposed of by an equally supernatural reconciliation.
On the other hand, there is the devoted attendant
of later years, who cannot be detached from her
mistress by any persecution or abuse and who feels
to the full the peculiar and almost magnetic charm
which she undeniably exercised over those who were
qualified to respond to it. As this woman says:
'Since God made her love known to me, nothing
has satisfied me but her, and wherever she has
gone, I have stretched my utmost steps to keep
pace with her.' [8]

One asks oneself, how did this lady fare in the
other practical concerns of life? She herself tells us
that she was simple as a babe in such affairs, yet
when divine wisdom spoke through her, her judgment was found singularly valuable. In money
matters she professed and apparently felt a considerable indifference. She was born wealthy and
indeed complains that she had never known the
blessings of poverty. When it comes to business
transactions, she again bewails her utter natural
incompetence, yet again, when a higher power
comes to her aid, she displays an acumen and a
gift of vigorous and accurate handling which as-

tonish even skilled men of affairs. In regard to one intricate negotiation she says: 'I was extremely surprised to see that I understood all the complications and subtleties of this business without ever having studied them, and the chief judge was so astonished at something so different from what he had expected that he conjured me to see the other judges and explain things to them at once.' [9] Whatever harmless vanity there may be about this, there is no question but that she used her wealth widely and freely for the service of others, and was ready to give her time, her strength, her pride, and her patience to relieving suffering and misery of all sorts.

Nor was she inclined to spend money on herself or her own indulgences. In her youth she was beautiful, had singular charm of manner and expression as well as of feature, and her tender conscience frequently reproached her with her attention to her mirror and her disposition to ornament her person and to make the most of it in every way. But constant ill-health no doubt somewhat undermined the physical attraction and the culmination of this in a siege of smallpox deprived her of all pretensions to regular beauty, though the attraction probably remained more than she admitted.

From that time on she cultivated her soul and let her body go, or thought she did.

It is hardly likely, however, that at any time the pleasures and distractions of this world had any great hold upon her. Its larger interests apparently never meant anything to her at all. In all the vast number of printed words that flowed from her there seems to be no recognition at all of politics or art or speculative thought or even of the beauty of nature. In her higher and remoter world these things simply had no existence. Nor did the ordinary amusements of life make much more appeal to her. Games and the theater are merely left out. She mentions with shame that there was a time when she danced, but it was a very brief time indeed. Any one who wrote with such immense facility must have had some gift with the tongue, and no doubt she could talk readily and well, but her precepts for conversation, which she recognized as being 'the social basis of life' savor more of the amiable than the piquant: 'Never speak of your neighbor except to his advantage, taking as far as you can the part of the absent who are abused. Never pass judgment on any one and be not quick to believe the evil that is told of others. Do not falsify and do not exaggerate.' [10]

In short, she was a saint, she really and undeniably was, and saints are not always the most agreeable people to live with, at any rate for those of another complexion, which perhaps explains the business of her parents, and her husband and mother-in-law, and her children. The saints are profoundly and first of all impressed with the necessity of setting an example and doing one's duty. Admirable as these motives are and indispensable as they are for the uplifting of the world, they do not always make comfortable housemates for those who have no desire whatever to set an example to any one and who feel, with the lady in the French comedy, that one's duty is something one is so glad to have done — because one has not got to do it again.

II

But Madame Guyon is to be regarded, she regarded herself, as a child not of this world but of the other, one of those exceptional beings who have a constant sense of the unreality of the real, of the complete insignificance of all those little overwhelming daily trifles which to the mass of us common men and women seem immensely — and so temporarily — significant. She was born with this tendency inherent in her and all her circumstances and surroundings encouraged and fostered it. Her brooding, sickly childhood made her introspective. The unresponsiveness of her family drove her in upon herself. The conventual training, which would have fretted and irritated some spirits, Ninon for example, exactly suited her, brought out all the peculiar elements of her nature. If she heard about the martyrs, she immediately wanted to be a martyr herself and thought that God probably intended her to be one. If any accident befell her, it was sent for her discipline and purification and the manifest interference of divine power prevented it from being worse than it was.

Her education, such as she had, was of just the easy and slipshod quality that fitted her temperament. She read vastly, and all sorts of authors, at least if we are to accept her own account. At any rate there can be no question as to the variety and extent of her religious reading. She learned Latin that she might have wider access to theological authorities, and Latin was an unusual accomplishment for a girl in that day. She read the Bible with extreme and constant zeal and early applied her own ardent ingenuity in subtle interpretation of it. She read the great mystics, Saint Teresa, Francis of

Sales, Catherine of Genoa, John of the Cross, Molinos, and absorbed their strange reveries with remarkable analytical understanding and still more emotional sympathy.

She had renewed experiences — one is almost tempted to call them shocks — of conversion. They came in her girlhood, they came when she had begun to get out into the world, they came with persistent force when she had contracted the obligations and burdens of her unfortunate marriage. Finally they were so compelling and the trials and difficulties of the earthly marriage were so great, that she executed a formal document by which she bound herself as loyal spouse to 'our Infant Lord,' entreating that he would grant her as 'the dowry of her spiritual union, crosses, contempt, confusion, opprobrium, and ignominy, and I implored him to give me grace to enter into his true disposition of humility and self-annihilation.' [11]

It is profoundly curious to analyze and follow the inward process of development which accompanied this external growth of religious experience. There is first the uneasiness, the vague longing, the unrest, the divine discontent with aught but the eternal and the desire to find in life something that mere earthly contacts and pleasures and interests can never yield. The effort to satisfy this is apt to take, with Madame Guyon in the earlier days it did take, strange and abnormal forms. She practiced all sorts of self-torment, of privation, of fantastically imposed and distressing discipline. Even in her childhood she used to go without her breakfast every morning and hide it behind the altar as an offering to the Lord.[12] She pinned a paper on her skin with the name of Christ written upon it. She endeavored to mortify herself by practices hideously offensive to a delicate taste like hers and really too disgusting and repulsive to be written down.

Then she discovered that these methods of extinguishing this world were crude and violent and though she never wholly admitted their inefficacy, she turned to what was subtler and finer and more spiritual. The great, the supreme agency, the unfailing agency for her, was prayer. And here again, after employing prayer in daily matters and common human needs, after making her ordinary conduct and that of others a matter of divine counsel and inquiry, she came to appreciate that the real function of prayer was something higher and deeper and purer. No doubt her ideas and habits on this subject were derived from the earlier mystics, but she amplified them and subtilized them in a fashion of her own, and the most notable and widely read of her books is that on a 'brief and very easy method of praying.' In other words, she believed that while mere vulgar, material petition might have its place, the prayer that really counted for the sanctified soul was that of contemplation, of laying aside earthly desires and petty interests, and losing yourself completely in communion with the divine. But no words at my command will equal hers for conveying the matter with vividness and delicate tenuity: 'I have been taught how the angels contemplate.... The soul, raised above all common possibility, admits no distinct view nor object, but is absorbed in the superessential God. It is a condition that surpasses all understanding. I have learned the necessity of admitting no thought, of any nature whatsoever, either good or bad, and that one must be detached from every bond, if one is to enjoy prayer in all its purity.' [13]

Thus, by the aid of this impersonal, immaterial prayer, and by rising above the trammels of earthly need and even of earthly torment, she soared to the heights of spiritual ecstasy, which are more or less known to all the mystics and are so difficult for the profane to understand or penetrate. She reached the doctrine of '*pur amour*,' love untainted by self-interest, which Fénelon so fully amplified after her and which Voltaire gently mocked when he spoke of 'the great Fénelon who believed that God could be loved for himself alone.' Madame Guyon at any rate believed it and with one of the most passionate spiritual efforts of the world she built her life on it.

Naturally the experience, as we find it in Madame Guyon, does not differ from the expression of it in earlier mystics and in later. There is no richer or more ardent exponent of it than Saint John of the Cross, who says: 'My will passed out of itself, became divine, because, being united with the divine love, it loves no longer with the limited force and vigor with which it loved before, but with the power and the purity of the spirit of God.... And in short all the forces and affections of the soul, by means of this darkening and eliminating of the old Adam, reawaken and are changed into a glory of divine delight.' [14] And Madame Guyon's expression is not far behind that of Saint John. 'There is nothing great, there is nothing holy, there is nothing wise, there is nothing fair, but to depend wholly upon God, like a child who does and can do only what he is bidden.' [15]

It is not to be supposed that with the saints, at any rate a saint like Madame Guyon, these raptures of spiritual ecstasy are permanent, or pervade the whole of life. On the contrary, as one surveys her career, one gets a general impression of unhappiness and dissatisfaction, not only of tumult and turbulence in her external existence, but of restless disquiet and even misery within. She herself dwells upon the long years when she yearned for peace and communion with God and could not obtain it, and though she indicates that in the end she did obtain it and retain it, the possession would appear to have been by no means untroubled or secure. She herself points out to a disciple that, no matter how sanctified one may be, one must 'expect all one's life to suffer these vicissitudes,' [16] these astonishing, inexplicable depressions and exaltations, these periods of abandonment, of desolation, of aridity, of spiritual despair.

What is perhaps most noticeable in her discussion of all these spiritual states is the richness and variety and delicacy of vocabulary with which she treats them. Long before her time the great mystics had invented a verbal technique for their own use, coining words with obscure psychological intent and value, or employing usual expressions in a strange and novel sense. Madame Guyon avails herself of all these novelties of her predecessors and adds to them many special verbal adaptations of her own. Thus one is surprised to find her introducing such thoroughly modern laboratory slang as 'introvert' and 'extravert.' [17]

And in general one is almost bewildered by her enormous flood and facility of words. Writing seems to have come to her almost as easily as breathing. She poured out book after book with apparently limitless abundance and it must be confessed with a singular fluency and often even grace. She herself of course disclaims any literary ambition or any literary skill whatever: it was not her own work, but the divine power working through her. Yet, wherever she got it, she unquestionably had it. Her complete works, in the most extensive edition, fill forty volumes. There are twenty volumes of commentary on the Bible, various volumes of poems, many of them delicate and charming, and curiously enough setting the abstract passion of mysticism to popular secular airs, many solid volumes of Spiritual Letters, besides the few more formal works which were supposed to contain the quintessence of her doctrine.

And with the verbal facility there is also a striking depth and delicacy of spiritual observation and analysis. This dreamer, this wide wanderer in un-

mapped intellectual worlds, had a close and keen
insight into the mental complications not only of
her own soul but of the other souls that worked and
played and battled about her. Henry James loved
to distinguish and disentangle what he called
'shades.' This mystical lady had no less a love than
he for the minute, the subtle, the evanescent move-
ments and shiftings and complexities of the spiritual world.

Yet the general impression derived from turning
over this vast work is one of almost desperate monotony. Voltaire said of Petrarch, 'He is the genius
of the world most skilled in the art of saying always
the same thing.' [18] But Madame Guyon carried the
process even further than Petrarch. She was so
absorbed with the one thing needful that all the
needless things that make the charm of life and
especially the diversity of literature slipped by her
unperceived. And when you distill the essence of
her work, it comes down to a few very limited ideas,
repeated over and over with extraordinary fertility
of variation.

It is true that the subtlety of the process sometimes suffices to conceal its tenuity. She traces the
slow development of the spiritual life through manifold, elaborate degrees with the most patient, deli-

cate analysis, and with a complexity of distinction
which makes saintliness seem a fine art beyond not
only the practice but even the comprehension of
common mortals. Yet the various stages of growth
may perhaps be simplified and suggested in a tangible and not unintelligible form.

After the first stage of restless uneasiness and
vague longing comes the realization that the only
way to deal with one's self is to get rid of one's self.
First the passions and desires must be rooted out,
trodden under foot, forgotten as if they had never
existed. But you must go deeper, you must strike
down to the foundation of the passions in the will,
and that too must be mastered and completely
overcome. And as the aspiration heightens and
strengthens, the intensity of renunciation and sub-
dual becomes more overwhelming and supreme.
Destruction, annihilation, nothingness, absolute
death are the words Madame Guyon reiterates, in
her passionate effort to convey the complete elimi-
nation of self that she preaches and teaches. Language is wrested and wrenched and twisted and tortured, in the struggle to express the inexpressible,
as in the following: 'You ask, why this process? It
continues from the commencement of the way of
life to the very end, to make the soul pass from the

multiple to the distinctly sensible without multiplicity, then from the distinctly sensible, to the distinct insensible, further to the sensible distinct, which is a general perception much less sensible than the first. This perception is vigorous at the beginning and introduces the soul into the essence of the perceived, which is a purer and stronger perception than the former. From this essence you pass into the enduring and the active power of love, thus moving from the sensible to the spiritual, and from the spiritual to pure faith, which, teaching us to die to even the life of the spirit, makes us die completely in ourselves and enter into God, to live in future in the divine life only.' [19]

No doubt it seems like a haze and mist and chaos of words. Yet you feel that the woman was striving to get at something and dimly and obscurely and almost divinely getting at it. The destruction of self was a real, a vital thing to her, and even more real, beyond such destruction, was the loss, the merging, the dissolution, the absorption of self in God. Over and over she returns to the figure of the petty streams that lose themselves in the ocean, to illustrate the complete divine submergence of the transfigured self: 'It is to be noted that the stream or torrent thus precipitated into the sea does not lose its own nature, though it is so changed and so lost that one knows it no longer. It is always what it was, but its existence is submerged and lost, not in its reality, but in its quality; for it assumes so much the quality of the ocean wave that you can see nothing in it peculiar to itself, and the more it sinks, is buried, and swallowed up, the more it forfeits its own quality to take that of the sea.' [20] And again, without figures, she endeavors in wonderfully sublimated speech to suggest the intensity of the union of the unselfed self with pure Deity: 'The soul is no longer either confined or possessed, nor does it possess or even enjoy; it perceives no difference between God and itself, sees nothing, possesses nothing, distinguishes nothing, even in God. God is the soul and the soul is God.... It is not even as if there were only God and the soul, that is not it, but it is as if God were alone, for the soul neither thinks God, nor perceives God, nor is grateful to God, nor desires anything whatever for itself at all.' [21]

III

The cardinal principle, the essential element of this spiritual progress is evidently the denial of self, and it is in the highest degree curious to see how, in the case of Madame Guyon at any rate, self is renewed and resurrected in the instinct, the passion for communicating one's religious experience and so influencing, controlling, dominating others. With Madame Guyon this is so marked that the French psychologist Seillières has written an extensive book pointing out and analyzing the contradiction between her theories and what he calls the 'imperialism' of this dominating, self-asserting, thoroughly egotistic instinct. Anatole France summed up the same instinct in one brief, comprehensive touch, when he spoke of 'la douceur impérieuse des saints,' 'the imperious gentleness of the saints.'

There are two very different types of saintliness. There is the purely inward type, which concentrates its spiritual effort, its spiritual existence, wholly upon the relation between itself and God and is very little concerned with the same relation as it affects others, or leaves the development of that relation to them. This type appears in the Author of the 'Imitation,' or among women, in Saint Catherine of Genoa, as a later example in Eugénie de Guérin, or to come nearer home to ourselves, in such a wayward but genuine mystic as Emily Dickinson. These souls are content to dwell with

God in a white silence of their own, 'like a shut rose all day turning their thoughts within.' The other type is not for a moment satisfied with its personal salvation, but is bent, bound, to scatter the good news abroad among all nations, to spread wide the splendid beneficence among the millions who are so woefully in need of it, and incidentally, if quite unconsciously, to fulfill its own ambition, its own thirst for power, in the process. This fascinating blend of philanthropy and self-assertion, mingled in varying proportions, is everywhere evident in natures like Ignatius Loyola or Saint Francis of Sales; it shines out vividly in all the ancient apostles and modern evangelists, it is conspicuous for example in a temper like that of D. L. Moody, and it is perhaps peculiarly congenial to the missionary instinct of women. Certainly it is characteristic of Madame Guyon, as in the America of recent years it flared out triumphantly in the life and work of Mary Baker Eddy, and is epitomized in her concise outcry to her satellite Richard Kennedy: 'Richard, I was born an unwelcome child and I mean to have the whole world at my feet before I die.'[22] This instinct of domination was no doubt born in Madame Guyon, as all our instincts are. But in earlier years it was hesitating and timid. As she came to see her own way more clearly, to formulate her own relation to the world and to God, she was more and more possessed by the impulse to communicate her discoveries to others and let them profit.

Naturally a temper so sympathetic and responsive was immensely influenced by others as well as inclined to influence them. In early years there was a certain Madame Granger, to whom Madame Guyon turned for spiritual advice and assistance, and one confessor after another moulded and kneaded her spirit, and incidentally was moulded in turn, perhaps more than he appreciated. But the first, commanding influence was that of Père La Combe. La Combe was himself a mystic of an advanced and subtle type, richly impregnated with the ideas of his predecessors. Many of these ideas he imparted to his eager pupil, and again he was affected and stimulated by her. It is clear that Madame Guyon was not very discreet in her relations with him. They traveled about together, not alone, but in a fashion sufficiently intimate to cause comment, if not scandal, and in his later years of imprisonment, persecution, and final madness, La Combe was supposed to have furnished confessions which put their relation in a most unfavorable light. No one who has studied Madame Guyon will doubt her for a moment, but it can hardly be said that the association with La Combe was wholly beneficial to her. On the other hand, the influence of Fénelon, who came later, was beneficial in the highest degree, more so to her than to him, sobering and clarifying the extravagance of her ideas and giving them the human bearing which she herself could not always impart.

But what others did for her is unimportant beside what she did for them, and it is undeniable that not only her doctrines but far more, as with Mrs. Eddy, something infectious and magnetic in her personality stirred souls, touched them, inspired them, lifted them out of themselves. And it is pretty to see how she deprecates the office, protests that she does not seek it, finds it a care and a burden, even while it is evident at every moment that it is the breath of life to her, as it was to Mrs. Eddy or to Moody: 'O God, what have I done to you that you should load me with souls after this fashion? Have I borne them in my womb that you should seem to wish to make me pay all their debts?' [23] And again: 'Alas! Formerly I thought only of God and tasted in him perfect peace; but since he has charged me with the welfare of my neighbor, all the wounds that that neighbor receives from his enemies or from himself, who is the greatest of his enemies, beat right upon my heart.' [24]

And so all classes of souls seemed to be under her care, provided she could get to them and touch them. It might be a servant, or a working-man, or a casual acquaintance. What matter, if she could drop a seed that would germinate and flourish? And again, moving as she was privileged to do, among the highest of the great world, she approached them also, and neither rank nor riches proved any barrier against the gentle suavity of her touch. Some of the very greatest people of her day came under the charm, like the two sister duchesses of Beauvilliers and Chevreuse, and through them the two dukes, who by their control over the heir to the throne of France were among the most important persons in the kingdom. For a time Madame Guyon's doctrines made their way into Madame de Maintenon's pet school of Saint-Cyr and even considerably affected Madame de Maintenon herself. But that calm, collected, self-poised spirit had by nature little use for raptures and ecstasies. When she found whither Madame Guyon was leading, she hesitated, faltered, and her defalcation was the most marked symptom in Madame Guyon's decay and disaster.

For it was the instinct for influencing others that was the cause of all Madame Guyon's troubles. If she had been content to enjoy God for herself, in peace and silence, the world would never have heard of her, she would have had no tragedy — and no glory. But when she began to spread and teach doctrines that ran right counter to the easy, self-indulgent common sense of common men, the powers of the world, both religious and secular, assailed her in all their congregated might.

As usually happens, they first attacked her morals. In spite of her indiscreet treatment of Père La Combe and of his dubious revelations, it was hardly possible to arraign her very seriously on the ground of personal weakness. But with doctrine it was a different matter. All the mystics, in their passionate effort to overcome the self, both for good and for evil, laid themselves open to the charge of neglecting moral distinctions. Madame Guyon, like her predecessors, always took it for granted that a soul that was given to God could do nothing that God would find displeasing. But everywhere in her writings there are ambiguous phrases that might easily mislead, unless they were spiritually interpreted. For example, 'God does not destroy the virtues as virtues; but he destroys our proprietorship of these same virtues.' [25] Or again, with the infinite subtlety so characteristic of her: 'When you find fault with me, you will notice that I almost always excuse myself. That is because the faults have no real existence and when I look for them, I do not find them, since in a creature like myself there is no longer any proper substance, so that faults do not make any impress, as they do with other souls.' [26]

It is not necessary for us to enter into the details of the miserable Quietist controversy, which spread far beyond Madame Guyon. But on these moral and doctrinal grounds she was involved in it, most distressingly. She was repeatedly examined and interrogated. Her writings were put under the ban. And after being at first restrained with more or less moderation, she was finally imprisoned in the Bastille. The whole affair had all the disagreeable savor that attends religious dispute. Even the noblest and finest spirits were soured and corrupted by it, and as Jules Lemaître aptly remarks, it is pitiful to see 'so much hate about pure love.'

The central figure in the attack on Madame Guyon was unquestionably Bossuet, and Bossuet was one of the most high-minded as well as one of the purest spirits that France has produced. But in this matter he, like his antagonist Fénelon, who supported Madame Guyon, would seem to have been influenced by motives that were sometimes too human to be altogether creditable. In any case, he had no sympathy whatever with Madame Guyon's attitude and summed her up as a woman 'whose knowledge was limited, whose merit was slight, whose illusions were palpable,' [27] or again, even more effectively, 'she prophesies the illusions of her heart.' [28] He, like Madame de Maintenon, belonged to the type of clear, practical common-sense intelligences, to whom the vague emotions of mysticism meant little, for whom pure love, the devotion of a soul which had no regard for its own welfare, even in heaven, but accepted the will of God, though it might lead to hell, was pure non-sense, and over whom consequently Madame Guyon had no lasting influence.

But there were plenty of others over whom her influence was profound and endured to the end. She herself marks sharply and repeatedly the distinction. 'There are souls,' she says, 'which do not belong to me, to whom I say none of these things. But for those which are given to me, like yours, God, by binding them to me intimately, gives me the knowledge of what is suited to them and of

the designs he has for them.' [29] To appreciate the
depth, the delicacy, and the power of this influence,
one should look over the vast length of the Spiritual
Letters. Monotonous as they in a sense are, and
harping continually on one or two notes, they show
an extraordinary passionate interest in the spiritual
life of others and a gift for ordering and developing
it almost like that of Saint Francis of Sales or of
Fénelon himself. Those who are in distress or
despair she comforts, those who are negligent or
forgetful she rebukes, those who are lukewarm or
hampered by the world she cheers and stimulates
and inspires. And always, always there is the confidence of a heaven-born prophet in her own mission
and her own power: 'Yet Our Lord, together with
all the weakness of childhood, gives me the power
of a god over souls; so that with one word I can put
them in torment or in peace, according as it may be
best for their eternal welfare.' [30]

By far the most notable among those who were
influenced by Madame Guyon, the disciple indeed
who gives her her main importance in the history
of France as well as in the history of religion, was
the great Fénelon, Archbishop of Cambrai. Fénelon
was one of the most complicated as well as one of the
most fascinating characters that ever lived. With

all the ardor, all the loftiness, all the spiritual purity
and abnegation of a saint, he combined a warm, intense, supple, subtle humanity, mobile, flexible,
now exalted, now depressed, now self-confident and
now distrustful, able in the highest degree to guide
and direct others, yet at the same time feeling that
no one was more in need of guidance and direction
than himself.

What Madame Guyon did for Fénelon, both for
good and evil, is altogether inestimable. She, quite
inadvertently, thwarted his ambitions and ruined
his worldly life by involving him in her cause and
interests; but spiritually, if she did not make him
what he was, she at least developed much that
might have been latent without her. She to some
extent, as it were, crystallized him doctrinally, but
this was of far less value than the support and en-
couragement that came to him from her magnificent
assurance and her confident hope. The relation between them is hard to define. The difference of sex
of course entered into it to some extent, as it always
does in such cases, though to put it on the level of
any ordinary, even Platonic, sexual connection
would be absurd. The language in which Madame
Guyon expresses her intimate nearness to this
chosen disciple of her heart has an extraordinary

compelling intensity of spiritual penetration and Fénelon's own account of it is not far behind. Thus, Madame Guyon writes: 'It is an intimacy which cannot be expressed, and unless we should be made of one substance, there could not be anything more near. I had only to think of him to be brought nearer to God, and when God enfolded me most closely, it seemed to me that with the same arms that enfolded me he also enfolded him.' [31] It is rare that we get such an inward display of the spiritual relation of two great souls.

It is to be noted that Madame Guyon's attitude in this matter of influence is that she herself is of no account and the power of God behind her is all. She insists again and again on her poverty of spirit, her ignorance, her incompetence. By herself she can do nothing. Her human will is poor, feeble, inept, and blundering. It is only when she resigns her own will and accepts the will of God as the directing force that she can accomplish great things, in fact anything. No doubt a question arises in the mind of the profane outsider as to just how you are to distinguish your own will from God's. Such a suggestion is unavoidably conveyed in Madame Guyon's tremendous statement: 'As to obedience, you (God) taught me to practice it with the submission of an infant; but also how far have you yourself obeyed, or rather, have you rendered my will marvelous by making it pass through your own.' [32] In other words, the ego, by renouncing itself, gains an enormous acquisition of power in getting the whole directing force of the universe behind it. I was repeatedly struck with this subtle transposition in the case of D. L. Moody, and there can be no more triumphant display of it than the exultant prophetic outcry of Madame Guyon: 'The Lord will one day pour forth his pity; he will establish the lines of his empire through me, and the nations will recognize his sovereign power. His spirit shall be diffused through all flesh: my sons and my daughters shall prophesy and the Lord will take delight in them. It is I, it is I, who in all my weakness and my littleness shall sing the song of the Lamb, which is sung only by the virgins who follow him everywhere.... Yes, I shall be through him the mistress over those who rule, and those who are subject unto none shall be subject unto me by the force of his divine authority, from which they can never escape without escaping from God himself.' [33]

IV

But it would be wholly unjust to see in Madame
Guyon only an assertion and amplification of ego-
tism, and Seillière, in his desire to maintain a thesis,
emphasizes this aspect too much. When she faced
humanity, the sense of her own power may have
overcome her. But when she turned and faced God,
self and the ego were really forgotten, as much as
they ever are, and she surrendered herself to the
divine abandon and longing of the mystics, which
nothing but God can satisfy. No one exemplifies
more fully than she the cry of Amiel: 'There is but
one thing needful: to possess God.'

No doubt this mystical longing requires some
analysis, and there are various and complicated
elements present in it. There is certainly the suggestion of the element of sex, and modern psycho-
logy, with its everlasting sex-obsession, even endeavors to reduce all religious desire and ecstasy to
a more or less indirect sex basis. It cannot be denied
that much in the language of the mystics, especially
of the women saints, favors this interpretation.
Saint Teresa, Saint Catherine of Genoa, Madame
Guyon herself are always resorting to terms and
phrases that seem immediately borrowed from the
expression of impassioned sexual love, and it is

perhaps unfortunate that the more or less symbolical language of the Song of Solomon lends itself so easily to mystical uses, especially in such forms as Madame Guyon's Biblical commentary.

To solve this sex puzzle, we must look a little more deeply into the sex instinct itself. It cannot be reduced wholly to the mere physical, animal need, though such simplification so strongly commends itself to the processes of the laboratory. In all human love there is not only the physical element, there is the further complication of such strains as curiosity, the infinite vanity of admiration, the subtle assertion of the sense of power, the opposite feeling of abject dependence, each developing abnormally into what the laboratory calls sadism and masochism. But even deeper than these, so profound and fundamental that it seems sometimes to be what gives human love its entire significance, is the impulse to get out of oneself. Just as soon as the youth begins to think, he finds himself alone in the vast universe, shut off forever in the impassable barriers of this one isolated soul, from which he can never wander or escape. The first passionate tendency of reflection is to overleap the barriers, somehow, somewhere to get out of these everlasting limits, at any rate, to enlarge the soul, to deepen it, to enrich it. And the first suggestion for doing this is to strive to blend and merge it with some one of the other souls that it divines about it. This tendency mingles by instinct with the direct impulse of sex and the result is the complicated and elaborate physical and spiritual process which we call human love.

Now just this same longing and desperate effort for escape, for enlargement, is the basis of the desire of the mystic in religion, only here the desire is not confined to one individual, but has a wider reach, a vaster range, and aspires to lose and merge all personal identity in the infinite universe, in the all-embracing unity of God. This passionate desire, this unquenchable thirst for boundless release and limitless escape is no more evident in Madame Guyon than in all the other mystics of centuries before and after. It is as patent in the sacred books of the East as it is in Augustine and Ambrose, in à Kempis and Fénelon, in Emerson and Emily Dickinson. All alike they sum up their effort and their aspiring in the cry of the 'Imitation': 'And whatever is not God is nothing, and should be accounted as nothing.' [34]

The weakness, for the old, tormenting, analyzing intellect, lies precisely in that last touch. How are we to distinguish All from Nothing? The universe, as we know it, is but an eternal oscillation between unity and multiplicity, the one and the many. As Pascal puts it: 'Unity and multitude... it is an error to exclude either.' [35] But the mystic, in his intense desire for infinite enlargement and escape, will be satisfied with only the All, with absolute unity, and again, how are All and Nothing to be kept apart? In Schopenhauer's phrase: 'What remains after the entire abolition of will is for all those who are still full of will certainly nothing; but, conversely, to those in whom the will has turned and has denied itself, this our world, which is so real, with all its suns and milky ways — is nothing.' [36] And it is strange to see how, in the mystical madness of Madame Guyon, All and Nothing perpetually recur together and intimately blended, as if they were the two contradictory yet eternally interlocking keys of life and death. In her poems, in her letters, in her essays, always the refrain, All and Nothing, All and Nothing, each indispensable and each incomprehensible without — and with — the other. And with tragic complaint she deplores the reluctance of humanity to accept the combination: 'I know but one path, but one way, but one road, which is that of continual renouncement, of death, of nothingness. Everybody flies this way and seeks with passion all that makes us live; nobody is willing to be nothing, yet how shall we find what we are all seeking by a road which leads precisely wrong?' [37]

Yet, after all the analysis and criticism, there remains the mystic's rapture and ecstasy, which, as the best and greatest of the mystics convey it to us, would seem to be the most enduring, as well as the most fleeting of all the joys that exist. You may elucidate it, you may dissect it, you may mock at it. You can explain it, but you cannot explain it away. And for those who are privileged to feel it, it is apparently the supreme possession of the world. It peers out, cries out, in page after page of Madame Guyon, and if she has a passion for imparting it to others, it is mainly because she found it such a glorious refuge for herself: 'All other creatures, celestial and terrestrial, all disappear and vanish, and there is nothing left but God, as he was before the creation. Such a soul sees only God everywhere, and all is God to it, not by reasoning, or even by vision or illumination, but by absolute identity and unity, which making it God by participation destroys totally the vision of itself, and leaves nothing but God everywhere.' [38]

IV

EVE AND ADAM
MADEMOISELLE DE LESPINASSE

CHRONOLOGY

Julie-Jeanne-Eléonore de Lespinasse.
Born, Lyon, November, 1732.
Came to Paris, 1754.
Parted from Madame du Deffand, 1764.
Attachment to Marquis de Mora began, 1768.
Attachment to Comte de Guibert began, 1772.
Mora died, 1774.
Died, Paris, May 23, 1776.

IV
MADEMOISELLE DE LESPINASSE

I

SHE was one of the great lovers of the world. Like Sappho, like Héloise, like the Julie of Rousseau and the Manon Lescaut of Prévost, she knew the wildest torment of self-forgetful passion and ennobled it by the completeness of self-surrender, and she analyzed its subtlest tortures with an astonishing and revealing clarity. Yet at the same time she was a woman of the world, of the French eighteenth-century world, poised, self-possessed, dignified, keenly alive to all social forces, and keenly aware of their charm as well as of their hollowness. The contrast between the creature of social control and efficiency and the wrecked human spirit underneath is infinitely instructive and profitable. As Sainte-Beuve puts it, 'for a moment the veil is torn asunder, and we read bare soul.' [1]

Julie de Lespinasse was born in Lyon in 1732, the illegitimate child of the Countess d'Albon, who had also an older son and daughter by her husband. Julie's childhood was not unhappy until at fifteen she lost her mother. Her father married her older sister and for a time she lived in their family, not very comfortably. She was delivered from this by her father's sister, Madame du Deffand, who was blind, wanted a companion, and took Julie to Paris in 1754. At first things went smoothly. But the elder lady was proud of her salon and her social success. She was sensitive and jealous. And she soon saw that Julie was popular and was drawing altogether too much attention. They quarreled and parted in 1764, and Julie by the aid of friends set up a modest establishment of her own. This soon became a social center and she might probably have kept up an active and delightful career to old age, if it had not been for the strange complication of amorous disturbance, which we will elucidate more fully later and which shattered her whole soul before her death in 1776. All this earlier social portion of her history is well delineated in Mrs. Humphry Ward's novel, 'Lady Rose's Daughter.'

The tragic points of this unhappy life, no doubt at all times modified and affected by the sufferer's temperament, cannot be better summed up than in Mademoiselle de Lespinasse's own vivid and telling words: 'I who have known nothing but suffering and grief, who have been the victim of ill-nature and tyranny for ten years, who have no fortune, who have lost my health and have experienced only atrocities at the hands of those who should have given me comfort, and who had my childhood torn by the very care that was taken to cultivate and to heighten my sensibility. I knew terror and dread, before I had the power to think or to judge.' [2]

The main source of Julie's later sufferings may perhaps be found in her family difficulties. She had a deeply affectionate nature. She longed for love, yearned for love, and in the normal relations of life she did not get it. She was devoted to her mother's memory, and if her mother had lived, things might have been different. She would have been glad to turn to her sister and her brother, but they were unresponsive and manifestly preoccupied with their own interests. Julie's mother, when she was dying, gave the girl a considerable sum in cash and told her to keep it for herself. Instead, she turned it over to her brother, whether in actual surrender or in trust is not quite clear. At any rate, he absorbed it, and she heard nothing further of cash or gratitude. Such things do not foster family affection. She was devotedly fond of her sister's children, especially of Abel. Indeed, her love for children and her success with them are very evident, and children of her own would probably have solved her problems better than anything. Abel was always friendly, but when she turned to him for help in her troubles, he perhaps justly alleged that he had troubles of his own, and the best he could do for her was to effect a formal reconciliation with the Church when she lay on her death-bed. On every page that she wrote there is indisputable indication of her passionate desire to be loved and to love: 'I know only one pleasure, I have only one interest, that of friendship; that sustains and consoles me, but often also it tears me to pieces.'³

In her circumstances it would not be expected that she would have as many women as men friends. Yet there were women of high character and notable distinction to whom she was profoundly attached and who returned it. The beautiful, clever, and intelligent Madame de Boufflers was fond of her at all times. The Duchesse de Châtillon was a loyal and faithful friend. So discreet and judicious and refined a lady as Madame Geoffrin admired and sought Julie almost to the point of infatuation, and she showed her regard not merely in social attentions, but in the more solid form of an annual pension of three thousand francs which formed her friend's chief means of subsistence. But the most interesting and the most pathetic of these feminine relations is undoubtedly that with Madame du Deffand, and the connection would have been a source of lasting pleasure and solace to both, if the element of dependence had not entered into it. In the early days the elder lady spoke most highly of her young companion, and to a friend who praised her she said, 'When you come to know her better, you will see how much she deserves it; every day I am more and more pleased with her.' [4] They were both so intelligent, so noble, so really estimable, that they must have admired and loved each other.

But as a mistress Madame du Deffand's defects of disposition made her intolerable to a temperament at once so proud and so sensitive as Julie's, and when the break came, it was complete and irreparable. Julie was neither spiteful nor unforgiving, yet even she could never get over the treatment she had received. As D'Alembert says, in the portrait nominally addressed to her: 'You hate no one, unless perhaps one woman only, who has done all that could be done to make her hated by you.' [5] Madame du Deffand's wrath was more active and more enduring. She did her enemy a bad turn when she could, and she never refers to her without a sneer. Her comment to Walpole on

Julie's death is a touch of unrelieved ugliness: 'Mademoiselle de Lespinasse died last night;... it would once have been an event to me, to-day it means nothing whatever.' [6]

The chief element in Madame du Deffand's irritation and what continued to keep it alive was undoubtedly the personal popularity of her former dependent. The Salons then concentrated the social existence of Paris, always the most social city in the world, and no Salon was more popular than that of Mademoiselle de Lespinasse. Madame du Deffand attracted the literary men and scholars by her brilliant wit and her vast knowledge of life. Madame Geoffrin, by ample means of entertainment, by assiduous effort and judicious management, built up perhaps the most elaborate social fabric of all, but she was just a trifle too obviously the queen of it. Men and women visited Julie de Lespinasse because they were charmed by her. In her parlor there was no fear of a sharp tongue like Madame du Deffand's, there was no slight burden of control, as with Madame Geoffrin. Everybody said and did what he pleased, subject only to the limits of instinctive good taste. As La Harpe describes it: 'From five o'clock in the afternoon till ten you were sure of finding there the élite of all sorts, men of the Court, men of letters, ambassadors, foreigners of distinction, women of quality: it was almost a certificate of social standing to be received in such an assemblage.'[7]

The popularity of Mademoiselle de Lespinasse was not owing to her beauty. No one in passing her in the street would have picked her out as possessing any special attraction. Even her lover, Guibert, says that she was 'far from beautiful.'[8] She was over thirty when she broke with Madame du Deffand and set up her own Salon, but Grimm says that she had never been young.[9] Shortly after this the smallpox attacked her and decidedly diminished any attraction of mere feature that she may have had. Nevertheless, it is perfectly clear that she had an extraordinary charm that appealed to people of all sorts, to young and old, to rich and poor, to common and distinguished. The keenest analysts of her time endeavored to describe this charm, and if they did not succeed perfectly, their efforts are at least impressive. Thus, Guibert, in his eulogy of her under the name of Eliza, sums up admirably the play of her features, the infinite variety and swift mobility which made her seem to find a response for every sort of spiritual suggestion and approach: 'I have seen faces animated by wit, by passion, by pleasure, by despair; but how many subtle shades of expression were unknown to me till I met Eliza.'[10]   And D'Alembert suggests in her profoundly perhaps the surest method of making ourselves attractive to any one: 'If you please the world generally, you have especially the power of pleasing people who are worth it; and you please them by the effect they have upon yourself, by the delight which they feel in appreciating how much you grasp what is worth while in them; you have the air of being obliged to them for being agreeable, and thus you double the pleasure they have in being so.'[11]

If personal beauty was not responsible for Julie's success, money had even less to do with it. She did not depend in any way whatever upon those adjuncts and accessories of comfort or luxury which go so far toward social advancement when you are fortunate enough to possess them. Her meager income was too limited for any dependence of this sort. She was a shrewd and careful manager, and ran her simple establishment with all the frugal thrift of a prudent French housewife, yet, though the entertainment she offered her friends was intellectual and spiritual only, they willingly left the gorgeous apartments and splendidly furnished table of Madame Geoffrin to seek what Julie had to offer. She herself repeatedly disclaims the need of money and the desire for it: 'Paris is the place in the world where one can be poor with the least privation; it is only the tiresome and the foolish who require to be rich.' [12] And not only by her words but by her conduct she showed her indifference to riches, at any rate her unwillingness to acquire them by sacrificing either her independence or her pride. Never at any time did she seek, as her relatives feared she might, to assert her claim to a share in the family possessions. Yet ambitious as she was, no doubt she felt the lack of fortune, as any one would have felt it in her place.

It cannot be too much emphasized, however, that lack of looks and lack of money did not at all prevent her being a leader in the Parisian world. She had exquisite tact, adapted herself to the needs of every one, the wishes of every one, the character of every one. She let every one behave in her parlor with the utmost freedom, yet she had a remarkable gift of harmonizing all these different interests and making them center in her own leadership. She was not brilliant or witty like Madame du Deffand, did not abound in quick sayings or snapping epigrams, but the quality of her talk is excellently suggested by D'Alembert: 'What above all distinguishes you in society is the art of saying to each person just what is suited to him; and this art, though by no means common, is, as you practice it, perfectly simple: it consists in never speaking of yourself to others, but a great deal of them.' [13] And D'Alembert quotes a remark of hers, to the effect that she would like to know the weakness of every one, pointing out that this did not spring from cruel curiosity, but simply from the desire to meet every one's needs. [14] The result of this social gift is well indicated in the enthusiastic words of La Harpe: 'She inspired so much confidence that there was no one who at the end of a fortnight was not ready to tell her the history of his life. Hence no one had so many friends and every one of them was beloved as if he were the only friend she had.' [15]

This attraction appealed to the most notable people of the time as well as to the common and humble. Grave and dignified personages turned aside from their serious affairs to the diversion and sympathy that Mademoiselle de Lespinasse could offer them. There was the aged and brilliant President Hénault, long a faithful friend of Madame du Deffand, who remained loyal to her yet felt Julie's charm so much that he was said to have offered her marriage. There were the distinguished foreigners, like the Scotch philosopher, Hume, and the gay and clever Italians, Caraccioli and Galiani. There were popular authors like Marmontel and prominent statesmen like Turgot, who did more than almost any one to stay the oncoming tide of revolution, and who liked to discuss his plans and projects with the quiet Lady from Lyon. And there was the thinker and writer Condorcet, who put aside his own literary occupations to act as Julie's secretary and who remained her devoted friend as long as she lived. The extensive series of Julie's letters to him is most important in comparison with those to her lover, because the former show in eminent degree how wise, how sane, how thoughtful, how helpful she could be to all whom she cherished.

Among these great friends none was more constant or more useful than the philosopher and mathematician D'Alembert, who stood among the first writers of his time, with Voltaire, Rousseau, Montesquieu, Diderot, and whose literary influence was immense. In the early days D'Alembert had been a follower of Madame du Deffand, but when the young companion appeared, he immediately attached himself to her, was the most active leader in the revolt, and did not hesitate a moment when the older lady in a mood of foolish irritation told him that he must make his choice irrevocably.

Somewhat later D'Alembert was taken seriously ill. Julie at once went to his lodgings and cared for him. Also, finding that the lodgings were undesirable, she took him into the house where she herself lived, and here he remained until her death. Naturally this occasioned a certain amount of scandal, but those well qualified to judge assure us that there was no basis for it, that the relation was purely Platonic. At any rate, D'Alembert's devotion increased to the end, and Julie revered and admired him, in spite of her distraction to other and more passionate loves. Strangely, or perhaps naturally, enough, the philosopher never became aware of these, and he even pushed his blindness so far as to lay aside his own arrangements for the sake of tramping back and forth to the post office to fetch his friend's love letters. Only after her death, did he find out, by reading papers which she had implored him to destroy unread, that she cared for others more than she did for him, and this added unutterable bitterness to the lasting grief he felt for her loss.

Undoubtedly D'Alembert was the chief figure in

Julie's social success and the main agent in helping her to attain it, and through him she accomplished as much socially as she could ever have hoped or expected. Yet even in the days when she was most absorbed in the social whirl, and much more when she was overcome by a deeper passion, she felt the hollowness and emptiness of it all, its insufficiency to satisfy the needs of a serious spirit. She kept up the tumult to the end, yet in a moment of despair she cries: 'Good God! was there ever so much pride, so much disdain, so much contempt, so much injustice, in a word, the accumulation and mixture of all that has peopled hell and the mad-houses for a thousand centuries? All this was yesterday in my sitting-room, and the walls did not fall in!' [16]

II

For Mademoiselle de Lespinasse was as notable for intellectual force and insight as for social charm, and indeed a large part of the charm came from the clear and penetrating vision, always qualified by tenderness and spiritual grace.

Her education, as might have been expected from her circumstances, was no doubt of a rather rambling and uncertain character. Her mother probably gave her what she could, which was not much, and little else was given to her directly. Guibert tells us that she could read English and Italian. If so, it was probably more the result of her own assiduity than of any outside instruction. But the best training she could have was her quick wit and her vast and constant contact with the world. As she herself puts it: 'The President Hénault, the Archbishop of Toulouse, the Archbishop of Aix, M. Turgot, M. d'Alembert, the Abbé de Boismont, M. de Mora, these are the men who have taught me to think and to talk!' [17] She could hardly have gone to a better school.

She applied her keen insight and analytical power to the problems of life in general and too often with the melancholy which is apt to accompany such clear vision: 'I know very well that it is possible to cling more to one's own affection than to the person who inspires it, but when one comes to consider how little one really interests those for whom one would have given one's life, one is not indeed humiliated, but one is revolted, and such reflection must chill the warmest heart.' [18] She keeps up a close and constant observation of those about her, observation not really obscured by the depth of her tenderness and sympathy, though these qualities do conflict with it to some extent, as in her formal portrait of Condorcet. Above all, she profoundly, fearlessly, and almost cruelly analyzes herself, on all occasions and in all connections. Thus she dissects and explains her social attraction: 'I am loved only because people believe and see that it pleases me to be so. They love me for what I feel, not for what they feel. That proves at once the inadequacy of my intelligence and the activity of my soul.' [19] And again she lays bare the great spiritual gulf which neither social attraction nor anything else can fill or cover: 'My soul is dead to every sort of dissipation. There is a certain hour in the day when I wind up my moral machine as I wind my watch. And then, the movement once given, it goes more or less well. I hear people say that I am gay, and it delights me that, without a trace of insincerity, but only with the desire to keep people about me, I can conquer my natural disposition to the point of making the world think that I am gay. What is curious is that no one suspects the effort required to appear what I am thought really to be. But it is because people observe very little, and it is fortunate, for there is not much to be gained by seeing more than others do.' [20]

Also, the intelligence was not used merely in practical matters and in daily external contact.

Though she may not have had much formal education, Mademoiselle de Lespinasse was a wide and curious reader, and as in every other phase of her existence, she identified herself passionately with what she read. If the book interested her at all, she became part of it and made it part of herself. She loved Sterne, and consequently set herself to imitate him. Rousseau and Richardson took the profound and lasting hold upon her heart that they took upon so many eighteenth-century men and women, in some respects for good and in others not. Hear with what intense and poignant vividness she expresses this influence: 'If your heart is cold, if your mind is dissipated, you will think me mad. But withdraw for a moment into yourself. Read a letter of Clarissa, a page of Jean Jacques, and I will answer for it that you will understand my speech. Not that I pretend to arrive at theirs; but I dwell in the same country, and my heart is often in unison with that of the unfortunate Clarissa.' [21]

It might be supposed that such an ardent interest in literature, combined with daily association with great authors, would arouse a certain amount of literary ambition and desire to write great things of her own. This does not appear to any considerable extent. Julie occasionally wrote a formal portrait, and wrote it well. Also, the chapters intended to continue Sterne's 'Sentimental Journey' are cleverly done, though they would hardly be taken for originals. But Julie's ambition had another bent: she did not care so much to be an author herself as to have a hand in the making of authors. Her Salon was the headquarters of the literary politics of the day, and few days have been more political. Her friend D'Alembert was a prominent figure in the composition of the celebrated 'Encyclopédie,' one of the great literary forces of the eighteenth century. He was also an active member of the Academy, and no influence was more important than his in managing the affairs of that organization, which has always played so conspicuous a part in French and European literary life.

Julie entered with all her passionate soul into the politico-literary game. She toiled and cajoled and persuaded to get her friends advanced. And if she took no cruel or dishonorable steps against those who were not her friends, she at least experienced intense personal distress when they triumphed and her friends went to the wall. As the Goncourts admirably express it, in their brilliant account of Julie's Salon: 'It was there that party-successes were arranged, there that public eulogies were discussed and settled, there that the opinions of the day were dictated to posterity, there that was developed the philosophical despotism under which the Academy was ruled by D'Alembert.' [22]

It is easy to understand that the play and movement of this literary world, the complication of contending and conflicting passions and interests, and the feeling that the delicate threads might often be touched and guided by her little fingers should have gratified Mademoiselle de Lespinasse immensely. Brought up as she had been, an abandoned waif, a mere abject dependent, without name or friends or money or standing in the world, the relish of such gradually acquired success and popularity and influence must have been delicious. No doubt she enjoyed it fully and did all she could to retain it.

With politics proper it was something the same as with literature, though naturally Julie's direct political influence was little. Her intimacy with Turgot, who discussed with her his plans for reform, her acquaintance with the English minister, Lord Shelburne, and many others kept her familiar with what went on in governmental matters. Here, as elsewhere, her comments and opinions are intel-

ligent and original, even if they are not profound.
She was liberal and broad-minded, and imbibed
from Montesquieu the enthusiasm for the English
Constitution which was becoming fashionable in
the Paris of her day. But in politics, as in everything, the personal element with her is foremost.
She is passionately interested in the projects and
the success of her friends, and all that enthusiasm,
argument, and pressure can do to forward them is
done. And she takes everything home to herself,
infuses her own tinge of melancholy and appre-
hension into the course of public affairs as well as
into her private ones. In one anxious crisis she
writes of Turgot: 'For me, who have neither his
courage nor his virtues, I am penetrated with sadness and with terror. I believe all that I dread and
I think of the future only with anxiety.... Is it not
desolating to see that with a king who desires only
the good and a minister who has a passion for it, it
is evil that is done and that the great part of the
public wishes only evil. Yes, the ambassador is
right, in general we are a very poor lot.' [23]

Mademoiselle de Lespinasse's æsthetic interest
was not confined to books and authors, but extended to other aspects of artistic activity. And
here again what is notable is the intensely personal

quality of her enjoyment. She likes things because she likes them, because they touch her and move her, and the labored analyses of professional critics are very indifferent. In the curious essay called 'An Apology for a Poor Creature,' if it is indeed hers, she defends, or at least elucidates this æsthetic attitude with all her natural ardor: 'I beg you to observe that, if I exaggerate, at least I am never exclusive, and do you know why? It is because it is my soul that praises... and because, moreover, I am fortunate enough to enjoy to madness things that appear to be most opposite.' [24] And further: 'Let me say, let me repeat, that I judge nothing, but that I feel everything; and that is why you never hear me say "this is good," "this is bad," but I say a thousand times a day, "I enjoy"; yes, I enjoy, and I shall continue to enjoy so long as I breathe.' [25]

In painting she seems to have taken little interest, at least she rarely mentions it. But the theater charmed her, when it did not bore her. The intense and violent contrast of the two experiences appears characteristically in her comment on a play of Sedaine: 'The first two acts bored me to the point of not holding my attention, and the three last forced it to such an extent that I could not breathe;

and as attention is for me a violent state, I was dead that evening after it. My physical machine was worn out from the state of tension that had overcome my spirit.' [26]

With music, the excitement, the stimulus, the enthusiasm are even greater. She takes an intense interest in the dispute between the French and Italian schools, which agitated the whole Parisian world. But she frankly confesses that she likes them both, when they move her. And few things in the world move her like the music of Gluck's 'Orpheus'; it has power to help her for the moment even in her amorous despair: 'There is but one thing in the world that does me good, it is music; but it is a good that others would call agony. I wish I might hear ten times a day that air which tears me in pieces and brings back to me with ecstasy all that I regret.' [27]

Two of the most important emotional elements of life seem, either from temperament or from circumstances, to have been lacking to Julie. She had no enjoyment of nature, of the external world. In this no doubt she was like many men and women of her time. Still her indifference to the charms of country life is exceptional, even for the Paris of that day, and it is especially notable in the eager reader and admirer of Rousseau. She was a child of cities, she always dwelt in cities, and she loved them. When she did get away from the bustle and the pavements, she was anxious to get back.

Also, there is almost no hint in her writing of any interest in religion. God and the life in the future seem to offer her no hope or consolation at all. She lived with a horde of eighteenth-century philosophers, who had no care for these things, and she quite imbibed their indifference. One of the most curious external documents in regard to her, though her biographers take little notice of it, is the elaborate dialogue in which Diderot introduces her conversing on the secrets of the universe with the physician Bordeu, while their patient, D'Alembert, interjects various comments of delirium or dream. The attitude and opinions that Diderot gives her may not have much significance, but it is an extraordinary tribute that a man of his power should have thought her view of abstract matters worth presenting at all. In her own actual writing, however, God makes no figure, and if she refers to theology, it is to ridicule 'the folly of this absurd product of the human spirit.' [28] As to a life after death, eternal sleep appears to her the most natural solution and the most welcome.[29]

Yet it would seem as if few were born with more treasures of mystical passion and intensity to bestow upon the things of the other world. If God had got hold of her early, he would have possessed her completely and forever. As it was, the passion that she might have given to heaven was poured out upon creatures wholly of this earth, yet it cannot be denied that celestial strains were in it.

III

For under the varied normal surface of all these happily and properly varied normal human interests, there went on a hideous, magnificent, tragic tumult of volcanic amorous passion. And note that it was not the passion of a girl, but that it came to Mademoiselle de Lespinasse as a grown woman in her thirties, and swept her away as furiously as Juliet or Cleopatra. And when one stops to think of it, one wonders how many such passions are raging and swirling all about one, hidden and disguised as completely under the revealing feminine garb of to-day as under the more veiling habiliments of Julie's time.

First, to state briefly what the complication of her strange love entanglements was. In the earlier days, while she was with Madame du Deffand, there was an Irish adventurer named Taaffe, who seems to have aroused a suggestion of what was to come. But the elder lady broke this up, perhaps not untenderly, yet her interference was one of the elements in the breach that took place later.

Then, after Julie's Salon was well established, there came to Paris in the later sixties a young Spaniard, the Marquis de Mora. Mora was of the best family, and had before him a great career in either the diplomatic or the military world. He had been married, had a son, and had lost his wife, though he was much younger than Julie. His family naturally did not look with entire favor on his acquaintance with her, and their interference, together with his already failing health, acted as obstacles which perhaps did as much in a temperament like Julie's to kindle the flame as to quench it. She gave him her whole soul, and it is probable that he gave his in return, but it is not probable that there was any illicit relation between them, and marriage was what they both looked forward to.

The obstacles continually and almost hopelessly interfered with this. Mora was repeatedly obliged to return to Spain and in his absence Julie did little but think of him and write to him, though none of these letters have been preserved, the collection published in later years being undoubtedly spurious.

When Mora had left Paris for the last time, as it seemed incurably ill, Julie, who thought herself inconsolable, came into contact with the Comte de Guibert, a young soldier and author, whose recently published book on tactics had made him praised and admired and fêted everywhere. He seems to have had by no means the real worth or nobility of Mora, but he was brilliant, ardent, quick to understand and to respond, if also to forget. Julie insensibly began to confide her anguish to him, and almost before she realized, she found herself with another passion on her hands, as absorbing, as engrossing as the first, and terribly complicated with it. As the affair progressed, in a moment of complete abandonment, she made the last great sacrifice, which she had never made to her former, nobler lover, and from that hour on her life was a torture of tragedy and nothing else.

To complicate matters still further, Mora set out for Paris in a despairing effort to rejoin her, and died on the way at Bordeaux in 1774. Shortly after, Guibert put the climax on the whole tragic situation by marrying, professing to retain the most loyal friendship for Julie, who was all the time lavishing upon him a passion all the more frenzied because it was made up of such mingled elements, adoration, contempt, regret, remorse, despair, and fleeting moments of incomparable ecstasy. Human nature will not endure such extremes, and she died two years later, pouring out her soul to Guibert in the wild series of letters that have kept her alive for posterity, and at the same time never ceasing to cherish the memory of her earlier love.

Through it all the clear vision persists, and the curious torturing pleasure of analyzing one's sufferings to the minutest detail. Julie is constantly watching her experiences and applying her penetrating insight to the study of them. In this minuteness of agonized analysis it is interesting to compare her with our own American lover and sufferer, Sarah Butler, who dissected her love and her distress in the long series of letters which so often suggest Julie's.

Julie studied the feelings that love brought to her and exposed their inmost essence with an almost supernatural precision. When her lover is absent, she comments thus: 'It is not the length of your absence that afflicts me; for my thought will not dwell upon the extent of it. It is simply the present that weighs upon my soul, oppresses it, beats it down, saddens it, and hardly leaves it enough energy to desire a better frame of thought.'[30] She studies the exact relation that she bears to those she loves in all its phases: 'The difference between us is that you are at the end of the world and are quite calm enough to enjoy yourself. I am in Paris, I suffer, and I enjoy nothing. That is all there is to it.' [31]

With equal care and clarity she penetrates the feelings and the characters of her lovers and portrays them with extraordinary force and vividness. Most curious of all, though it will be quite comprehensible to those who have gone through a somewhat similar experience, she discusses one lover with the other and explains her passion to him who is not the recipient of it with an energy which must have been startling and not wholly agreeable. Again and again she tells Guibert how much she loved or loves Mora, for the love persisted even after his death, and she fortifies the love by the elaborate display of his admirable qualities. While she had still hope that he might survive, she expresses herself as follows: 'Consider whether it is possible to have a moment of repose when you are trembling for the life of one to whom you would at any moment sacrifice your own. Ah, if you knew how lovable he is, how worthy to be loved. His soul is gentle, tender, and strong. I am convinced that he is the man of the whole world who would suit you best.' [32]

And as she sees clearly the nature of her passion, so there are moments when she tries to overcome it, and to establish the calm, royal domination of her soul. She admires such domination. She is wise, and thoughtful, and helpful, in advising it for others. She writes to Condorcet, who had sentimental difficulties of his own: 'If you can attain repose and calm, believe that you have seized happiness. Alas! Is there any other? And can there be any when one has made one's existence dependent upon another? Were he a god, the sacrifice would be too great.' [33] Yet, even as she advises, she appreciates the absurdity of such good counsel coming from her, 'I who suffer without ceasing, I who know not how to calm myself, in a word I who have not common sense and can do nothing for my friends except love them tenderly and pity them with my whole soul when they suffer.' [34]

Then she determines to make herself over, to begin life anew with stoical serenity. She will not be ravaged longer by these tumultuous sins. She reads deep, edifying books, only somehow they do not take hold of her: 'I cannot read with interest: I am always reading what I feel and not what I see. Ah! how the mind weakens when one loves. To be sure, the soul loses nothing, but what is the good of a soul?' [35] Still, there are moments when she feels that she has succeeded, and triumphs in her hardly acquired serenity, but it is a rather lugubrious and mortuary triumph: 'For some days I had not the strength to suffer or to love. Then at last I recovered that degree of reason that makes one appreciate everything at its just value and makes me feel that if I have no longer any pleasure to hope for, I have at least no ill to fear. I have recovered calm, but I am not fooled by it: it is the calm of death.' [36]

It hardly lasts an hour. The tumult, the whirlwind, the hurricane of passion catches her and sweeps her away, breathless, a willing and consenting victim. Calm is death, and love, even if love is all suffering, at least is life. 'Oh, what pleasures, what delights a soul intoxicated with passion can still feel! My love, I know it, my life depends upon my madness: if I became calm, if I really gave myself up to reason, I could not live twenty-four hours.' [37]

The slightest whim of circumstance, the vaguest suggestion in her own soul or in his, is enough to scatter reason to the winds. Sometimes it is a fierce and sudden impulse of jealousy. Guibert was always attractive to women and only too ready to be attentive to them, much too attentive, at any rate in one case, as it seemed to Julie's anxious and suspicious heart. And, do the best she can, she will at times upbraid him and reproach him with it. Again Guibert is not so rich as he might be. The natural remedy for this complaint, in France, would be an advantageous marriage. Julie, in her saner moods, recognizes this, and she even looks out what she considers a promising and suitable connection and offers to do all she can to promote the match. But the gentleman, not unnaturally, prefers to do his own choosing, and almost unawares the despairing Julie finds her lover slipping out of her arms into the arms of another whom she is forced to admit to be in every way charming as well as rich.

And this ought surely to be the end. She ought to give him up, to forget him, to refuse with scorn the pale and decorous friendship which she feels is all that would be possible between them henceforth. But she cannot give up, she cannot let him

go. There is but one end possible for her, and life
and love have become so hopelessly intertangled
that never, never, never again can they be separated: 'Oh, heaven! how *terribly* one lives when one
is dead to everything except to one object which is
the universe for us, and which possesses our faculties to such a point that it is no longer possible to
live in any other moment than that in which one is
living.' [38]

And no doubt in this storm and tumult of passion and suffering the moments of rapture and
celestial ecstasy come and almost seem to pay for
all. As our old Spenser has it, in these love matters,

> A dram of sweet is worth a pound of sour.

Only sometimes it seems as if the sour came in tons
and floods rather than in pounds, and the drams of
sweet are very far between. But when they do
come, Julie recognizes them as frankly and as intensely as any one. Speaking of a lady whose lover
had been killed in a duel by her husband and who
was dying herself in consequence, she cries: 'If she
dies, or if she is dead, I do not pity her. Her lot has
been a happy one. She has known all the value of
life and has made it known to the one she loved. A
year of such a life is worth more than the century

of Fontenelle.... Ah! how rare such a love is! how great it is! how sublime it is! I honor it and I respect it like virtue.' [39] And her expression for her own case is equally ardent and convincing: 'Dear heart, with three words you make me a new soul, you fill me with an interest so keen, with a sentiment so tender and so profound that I lose the faculty of recalling the past and foreseeing the future. Yes, dear heart, I live wholly in you: I exist, because I love you; and this is so true that it seems to me impossible not to die if I should lose the hope of seeing you again.' [40]

The strange thing is that the currents of ecstasy and misery run side by side, often blending with each other so that you cannot tell which is which, and even it seems to require the misery to bring out and accentuate and complete the ecstasy. Such is the high-wrought and perpetually overstrained nature of those who live always in extremes. 'To love and to suffer, heaven and hell, this is what I would seek for myself, this is what I would live to feel, this is the climate in which I would dwell forever, and not in that temperate region which suits the fools and the automatons who are all about us playing and trifling with life.' [41]

Yet still remorselessly, through ecstasy and

through misery alike, there is the play of the incessant analysis, bringing eternal undeception and disillusion as to love, and most of all as to lovers. Even as to the nobler and better one, the disillusion would sometimes intrude, if we are to accept as genuine the portrait of Mora which is said to have been written by Julie during his life. While endowing him with all sorts of perfections, she yet suggests that these perfections are rather of the intellect than of the heart and that he is more framed to inspire love than capable of loving. But when it comes to Guibert, the criticism is unsparing, and the disillusion would appear to be complete. He is absorbed in himself, his only love is his ambition, his own glory, his own success. He is quite incapable of the entire abandonment and self-surrender which real love requires, does not care for it, does not understand it. And she brands him and she lashes him, till one comes to feel that a lamblike patience must have been at least one of his good qualities: 'Oh, my love! one should love you before knowing you, as I did; for when one comes to know you, it is like devoting oneself to hell to link one's happiness to such as you.' [42] She does not know whether she loves him or hates him most. 'You know that when I hate you, it is because I love you to a point of passion that unhinges my soul.' [43]

The real trouble through it all is that what she loves more than any earthly lover is an ideal, and what she longs for is so remote and so impossible that no earthly lover can realize it. It is the obscure consciousness of this that makes her tolerant of her lover even when she scourges him. And she is too well aware that she herself falls as far short of her ideal as any lover can do. It is the sense of her own faithlessness, her own disloyalty, that fosters the strange agonies of remorse which run like strands of molten metal all through the otherwise sufficiently glowing tissue of her letters. 'The past, the present, and the future offer me nothing but grief, regret, and remorse.' [44] So she speaks at the beginning, so she continues to the end.

This self-dissection, self-reproach, self-torment, even though blended with rare moments of unutterable ecstasy, keep her for the most part in moods of despair in which death is the only comfort and the only refuge. In both the ecstasy and the torment rest, repose, unbroken sleep seem immensely inviting and attractive: 'I am worn and weary with this voyage that is called life. I have not energy enough to terminate it abruptly, but I

see with relief that I am verging toward the end.' [45]
No doubt the spiritual condition was much ag-
gravated by physical weakness. Julie's health,
never robust, greatly shattered by the rough treatment received with Madame du Deffand, was
completely broken by this tumult of passion and
the fury of normal instincts repressed and distorted from their natural outlet. Through the
whole of her connection with Guibert she was obviously breaking and fading away, until she faded
altogether. And, like so many of her contemporaries, she had too often recourse to the disastrous
relief afforded by opium. Love, music, and opium,
she says, are the best remedies she knows for the
horror of life. And opium stupefied her, bewildered
her, and depressed her, more even than music or
love.

The natural, instinctive outlet for such abnormal
depression would seem to have been suicide, and
suicide was often in Julie's thoughts and sometimes
in her actual action. It was said that she tried to
take an overdose of opium after Madame du Deffand broke off the first love affair with the brilliant
Irishman. It is certain that she made the attempt
after Mora's death and was thwarted only by the
opportune interference of Guibert, an interference

for which she afterwards reproached him bitterly. But she made no further effort, content, for the next two years, to see the end more and more rapidly approaching. And to the very last she continued to write to her lover with the same strange blend of emotions, having forbidden him to see her, because her face was so distorted by her malady: 'Farewell, my Love. If I ever returned to life, I should like to spend it in loving you. But there is no longer time.' [46]

It must be admitted that through all this lengthy and at times monotonous record of suffering one gets a certain feeling of wilfulness, at least of intense subjectivity. The suffering seemed to be cherished and fostered, when an effort of active and practical common sense might perhaps have gone far to dissipate it. There is a suggestion of an artificial element, the brooding consciousness of Rousseau and Richardson, and perhaps just the least desire to be classed with them and to live in their world. Yet, after all, it may be that the sufferings of the imagination, when a stupid common sense is not efficacious to relieve them, are the most poignant and the most enduring. At any rate, it cannot be questioned that Mademoiselle de Lespinasse has left a record of love and wretchedness which few have equaled and none have surpassed. Let those who have known nothing whatever of the wretchedness or the love throw stones, if they choose. It is possible to gather together a pulsing climax of her brief, direct, passionate phrases which can hardly be matched elsewhere. They are simple, unadorned. No doubt words similar in intention are flying about us through the mails by the thousands every day. But Julie gives them a point and an intensity which we do not often see in print. 'I have only one thought, and that thought fills my soul and my whole life.' [47] 'There is but one interest, one pleasure, one misfortune, and one judge for me in the whole universe.' [48] 'I have no other interests, no other ties, no other friends, I have no need of them: to love you, to see you, or to cease to exist, that is the last, the only desire of my soul.' [49] 'I do nothing but love, I know nothing but love.' [50] Finally, there is the briefest and perhaps the completest love-letter in the world: 'At all the moments of my life: My Love, I suffer, I love you, I am waiting for you.' [51] So she goes out into the great night.

V
EVE ENTHRONED
CATHERINE THE GREAT

CHRONOLOGY

Sophie Auguste Frédérique, Princess of Anhalt Zerbst.
Born, Stettin, May 2, 1729.
Went to Russia at invitation of Empress Elizabeth, 1744.
Entered Greek Church and took name of Catherine, July 8, 1744.
Married Grand Duke Peter, August 21, 1745.
Empress Elizabeth died, January, 1762.
Catherine proclaimed Empress, July 9, 1762.
Peter murdered, July 17, 1762.
Rise of Potemkin, 1774.
Pugachev Rebellion, 1774.
Crimean triumphal progress, 1787.
Died, St. Petersburg, November 17, 1796.

V

CATHERINE THE GREAT

I

CATHERINE THE GREAT was born in a sleepy little German town, Stettin, the daughter of a sleepy little German prince. When she was fourteen years old, she went to Russia at the invitation of the Empress Elizabeth, married the heir to the Russian Empire, who was afterwards Peter III, dethroned him to save herself, and after his murder in 1762, became sole ruler, for thirty years, with varying vicissitudes, of the greatest empire in the world. She had limitless ambition, a long list of assorted lovers, an eminently cheerful temperament, and on the whole enjoyed herself vastly. What she herself thought of her career, or at any rate what she wished the world to think of it, is well indicated in the epitaph which she wrote for herself when she was sixty years old: 'Here lies Catherine the Second, born in Stettin, May 2, 1729. In the year 1744 she went to Russia to marry Peter III. At the age of fourteen she made the threefold resolution, to please her Consort, Elizabeth, and the Nation. She neglected nothing in order to succeed in this.

Eighteen years of tediousness and solitude caused her to read many books. When she had ascended the throne of Russia, she wished to do good and tried to bring happiness, freedom, and prosperity to her subjects. She forgave easily and hated no one. She was good-natured and easy-going; she had a cheerful temperament, republican sentiments, and a kind heart. She had friends. Work was easy for her; she loved sociability and the arts.' [1]

It seems fairer to Catherine to dispose first of the amorous aspects of her career. These form the best known and most conspicuous part of it for many persons, and after dealing with them we can turn to what is more solidly and permanently important.

When she came to Russia, at the age of fourteen, she assures us, and probably with truth, that she was innocent even to the point of being unaware of the nature of the difference between the sexes. When she was married, a year later, she was ready and anxious to love her husband, and again assures us, probably again with truth, that under happier circumstances, she would have made a faithful, devoted, domestic wife and mother.

Circumstances were not favorable. Peter was incapable of satisfying her, physically or mentally. He was perhaps not quite the drunken brute she represents him, but he was unbalanced, undeveloped, and fit to win from a creature like Catherine nothing but contempt. He got it, thoroughly, and she soon made up her mind that she must shape her life quite independently of him.

She craved affection as much as she craved power. The influences about her, from the Empress Elizabeth down, were utterly immoral, and the handsomest men in Russia courted her favor, while a handsome man was something she never could resist. According to her own story, after nine years of virgin marriage, the higher powers suggested to her that Russia must have an heir somehow. At any rate she drifted into a connection with Sergius Soltikov, who became the father of the future Emperor Paul. Soltikov was soon succeeded by Poniatowski, for whom Catherine seems to have felt a more romantic affection than for any one else. Poniatowski was devotedly attached to her and in his case the love seems really to have been for the woman as well as for the princess. In his delicate and sensitive description we catch something of the charm which, rather than any statuesque beauty, made Catherine widely attractive to all sorts of people: 'She had black hair, a dazzlingly fair skin, a brilliant complexion, large, eloquent blue eyes, long black eyelashes, a Grecian nose, a mouth that seemed made for kissing, a trim waist, not too small, an active and yet dignified carriage, a soft and pleasant voice, and a laugh as merry as her disposition.' [2]

Poniatowski might perhaps have stabilized that mobile heart. Unfortunately he was called away to be King of Poland, and Catherine was left to a long string of emotional vagaries. Poniatowski was succeeded by Gregory Orlov, one of the band of brothers who placed Catherine on the throne and disposed of her husband. Some years later, in 1774, Orlov gave way to that strange creature Potemkin, half genius, half charlatan, huge and physically unattractive, but the incarnation of power as well as of indolent self-indulgence. Potemkin's reign as an actual lover was comparatively brief, but he continued to be the Empress's soldier and minister as long as he lived, that is, almost as long as she lived, and the advice extended even to the rather singular office of suggesting his amorous successors, so that the Lanskois, the Yermolovs, the Mamonovs, were all Potemkin's creatures, until the unworthy and clownish Zubov engrossed Catherine's senile favor to her own discredit and the injury of the country. One notable thing about all these lovers is that

Catherine parted from them on the best of terms. She did not cut off their heads, like Henry VIII, she gave them huge sums of money and great estates.

Hat man die Liebe durchgeliebt,
Man fängt die Freundschaft an.

It is hardly worth while to list the whole varied collection in detail. Catherine's latest biographer makes specifically and exactly thirteen who possessed her heart, if heart it is to be called. I should regard any such mathematical precision as somewhat fantastic. But it is at any rate energetically to be insisted that the vast cloud of scandal that gathered about the 'Semiramis and Messalina of the North' in her own day and since is not to be completely accepted. There was no coarse or vulgar debauchery, no street-corner soliciting, no drunken riot. The solemn strictures that Sainte-Beuve, in his otherwise penetrating study, bestowed upon Catherine's morals may be well enough deserved, but, as in other similar cases, one cannot but feel that the French critic, in reprehending the freedom of others' conduct is making up for the extreme laxity of his own.

What interests us is not the gossip of the antechamber and the alcove, but what was Catherine's own personal attitude, how she herself really felt about her amorous adventures. In the first place it must be emphasized that in form all was respectable and decorous. Apparently she regarded the succession of love affairs as merely a series of companionate marriages, such as would delight the respectable Judge Lindsey and his enthusiastic followers. Or, one might set them down as a list of New York divorces, though perhaps thirteen husbands would be a trifle lively for even the metropolis of Manhattan. And Catherine was rigid as regards propriety. Light stories, risky anecdotes were discouraged and frowned upon. She reproved and punished her attendants for indiscretions which would have seemed to be similar to her own. The reigning favorite was established in a position of dignity and ceremony. He was given apartments next those of the Empress and his duties and privileges were settled with a formal routine which almost recalls the status of the Prince Consort with the late lamented Queen Victoria.

On the other hand, Catherine seems to have been blind or indifferent to the effect of her example in unhinging the marital relation through the country from top to bottom. She does not appear to have taken this into account, or, if she did, it did not weigh with her. She defended her own conduct with the strangely naïve comment that she was doing Russia a great service by training all these young men to be of use in the administration of their country. Of any sense of sin, of self-reproach, of such remorse and repentance as at times overcame Louis XIV, she does not show the faintest trace. From her childhood she had idolized Henri Quatre, the grandfather of Louis, and she seems to have felt that as Henri Quatre was a universal lover, she might be.

There are various passages of Catherine's own writing which are immensely significant as illustrating her moral attitude in this connection. Discussing her early frailties and the excuse for them in the Memoirs, written in advanced life, she says: 'For to tempt and to be tempted are things very nearly allied, and in spite of the finest maxims of morality impressed upon the mind, whenever feeling has anything to do in the matter, no sooner is it excited than we have already gone vastly farther than we are aware of.... Flight alone is, perhaps, the only remedy.... If you do not fly, there is nothing, it seems to me, so difficult as to escape from that which is essentially agreeable. All that can be said in opposition to it will appear but a prudery quite out of harmony with the natural instincts of the human heart.' [3] Still more curious is the letter written to Prince Potemkin, in 1774, when she was preparing to accept him in place of Orlov. In explanation and defense of her past vagaries she says: 'You will deign to see that there were not fifteen but only one third of that. The first, against my will, and the fourth, taken out of desperation, cannot at all be set down to frivolity. Of the other three only think rightly. God is my judge that I did not take them out of looseness, to which I have no inclination. If Fate had given me in youth a husband whom I could have loved, I should have remained always true to him. The trouble is that my heart would not willingly remain one hour without love.' [4]

Here I think we have the key to the whole strange, picturesque, or sordid epic wandering: it was still love and the search for love. It was no vain longing for a romantic ideal, but just the thwarted normal desire of an ardent and affectionate nature for some devotion in which it could rest, and this longing was more and more complicated by physical habit and need and especially haunted by the terrible doubt, entailed by her peculiar circumstances, as to whether she could ever be loved for herself alone.

Again I recur to the not unfounded, if rather amusing, strictures of Sainte-Beuve. What Sainte-Beuve cannot put up with is Catherine's lack of seriousness, her merry, animal, and at the same time thoroughly feminine enjoyment. There was never anything gay or merry about Sainte-Beuve and a healthy human merriment is largely the key to Catherine the Great. Her admiration of Sterne and Tristram Shandy is immensely significant. She thoroughly liked a good time, had the feminine appreciation of a handsome man, had the handsomest men in the world at her disposal, had a healthy body and vigorous, responsive senses, and always a feeling of imperial superiority to ordinary restraints. She liked to divert herself from the toil of government by a thoroughly light-hearted riot, and if the riot slipped into amorous and erotic indulgence, she did not in the least regret it. It is true that Tristram says no passion is so serious as lust, and probably Catherine took it seriously enough when it suited her, yet I am sure she contrived to mix a lot of laughter with it, and so to create an atmosphere as different from the morbid sexual analysis of Saint-Beuve as from the ideal strain of George Sand.

In love, as in everything, the clue to Catherine

the Great is to be found in this vigorous, cheerful, normal enjoyment of life. Her peculiar situation may have developed the enjoyment in erratic and not always commendable phases, but the joy in itself is infectious and fascinating. With her I am constantly reminded of the saying of a very different woman, Frances Willard, the great apostle of Prohibition: 'The chief wonder of my life is that I dare to have so good a time.'⁵ Or, in the more poetical and splendid words of Ninon: 'The joy of a soul is the measure of its force.'⁶ Now Catherine always, and justly, insists upon her capacity for joy. She was sometimes irritated, sometimes healthily unhappy from untoward circumstances. She was never melancholy, never brooding, in the sense of Sainte-Beuve's 'the soul of the voluptuous man is a burden to him.' She was a sound, healthy, normal, substantial, working woman, and as such we must follow her career in far other aspects than the merely amorous.

II

She was thoroughly a woman in the ordinary, daily, domestic concerns of living. I have no doubt she was at home in the kitchen, though I have no evidence that she could put on an apron and go out and cook, like Madame de Maintenon. Perhaps she was a little weak in this point, because she cared nothing about eating or drinking, being temperate in all such matters, and even abstemious, except for a passion for coffee and snuff, and no doubt the temperance accounted largely for the on the whole excellent health which carried her through sixty years of incessant and varied activity.

And Catherine had much of the prudent, orderly habit of the careful German housewife in the management of her ordinary concerns as well as of her great empire, *mon petit ménage*, she sometimes called it. She liked routine and system and practiced them. Her day was laid out with care and in the main the regular plan was followed. She rose at a definite, very early hour, had fixed times for reading, for working with her ministers, for receiving the innumerable persons who appealed to her for one purpose or another, and also for recreation and amusement. In one of her interesting letters to Madame Geoffrin she details this routine with delightful minuteness.[7] Again, in a letter to Grimm she takes huge credit to herself, with her usual grace of naïve self-commendation, for persisting in the workaday routine even when she was overwhelmed with grief for the loss of Lanskoi, the one of her later favorites whom she cherished with the tenderest regard: 'Do not imagine that, in spite of the horror of this situation, I neglected the least thing that really required my care. Even in the most agonizing moments everybody came to me for orders and I gave them with a clearness and intelligence which General Soltikov said impressed him immensely.'[8]

In money matters it must be confessed that, at any rate in early years, Catherine's systematic and successful management was less conspicuous. She was hurried from extreme German poverty to what seemed limitless Russian wealth, and for the time her head was a little turned. She spent profusely, she always liked to spend, and she got into serious trouble with the Empress Elizabeth because of debt. She hated niggardliness. 'I beg of you,' she said to a friend, 'do not propose to me candle-end economies. They might be suitable for some people, they are not for me.'[9] Above all, she liked to give and was at all times immensely generous, not to say lavish, not only to her favorites, but to those in real need. Yet in giving, as in living and in loving, she kept her head. She spent, she lavished, yet she never really squandered, and she had the vital instinct of always wanting to see where the money was coming from before she let it go. So that in the end she managed her personal finances, as she did those of her great empire, with skill and efficiency.

The Empress was again the thoughtful, careful, intelligent housewife in her treatment of those who served her. No doubt she was well and devotedly attended, but the most notable thing seems to have been her consideration. She hated to give trouble and avoided doing so when she could. One day she apologized to her guests for the food: the cook for that week, she said, was one who had been with her a good while and though he made wretched work of it, she could not bring herself to dismiss him.[10] Again, she took a company of friends on a sleighing party. They were all packed in to start for home when she discovered that the servants had not been fed, and she made everybody wait till this was remedied. She liked to get up early and lit her own fire so as not to disturb the maids at that unseemly hour. And there is the pretty story of the page. The Empress wanted an errand done and rang for a boy to do it. None came. She rang again, and again. Then, completely out of temper, she went to hunt up the culprit. She found him in an anteroom absorbed in a game of cards. Instead of scolding him, she watched the game, got interested, and told the boy she would play his hand while he did the errand.[11]

Catherine was all her life passionately fond of pets. Her families of dogs keep recurring in the letters to Grimm, with charming details of caressing and fondling. She loved her birds, she liked to feed the squirrels on the lawn, and when things went wrong, she paid a visit to her monkey. 'I never see him without laughing at him, he is such a mad creature.' [12] She was grateful to all creatures that made her laugh.

In her family relations she is much less attractive, perhaps because there was less laughter in them. Her sage and solemn German father she revered — at a convenient distance, and followed his advice when it suited her. Her mother escorted her to Russia and having notions and a character of her own failed to make herself agreeable to the Empress Elizabeth or indeed to her own daughter. She was finally packed home to Germany before the marriage took place and though Catherine shed some natural tears at parting, she got along much more comfortably without maternal supervision. She and her son and heir Paul never hit it off together. She got him two good wives and deeply bewailed the loss of the first one. She never actually quarreled with him, but their relations were far from affectionate. Nor was she much more interested in the son confessedly born out of wedlock. On the other hand, she was devoted to her grandchildren and her innumerable references to them in her letters are delightful. She spends endless of her busy hours in teaching them the alphabet, in teaching them the conduct of life, in teaching them the management of a great empire. She romps with them, she finds them playthings, she consoles their little distresses. She plans to have the elder succeed herself, without much regard to the intervention of his father, and for the younger, Constantine, she sets apart the dream empire of Constantinople, which was an object of revery and aspiration to her as to so many Russians since. I don't know that you can improve on her advice for training a great ruler, so far as it goes: 'Above all things, teach him to be beneficent and then inspire him with the love of truth. That will make him beloved by God and by men.' [13]

When we turn from these family tangles and complications to broader human interests, Catherine fully recovers all her charm. She liked people, liked to be with them, to study them, to dominate them, and she liked the occupations and amusements that brought her into contact with them. Indeed, she liked amusements of all sorts. Outdoor sport and athletic activity fascinated her. She would put on man's clothes, take a gun on her shoulder, and stroll off into the woods, to forget power with partridges, like Daniel Webster. She was an excellent rider, loved good horses, and herself tells us that she sometimes spent thirteen hours out of the twenty-four in the saddle, a man's saddle at that, much to the horror of the more conventional Empress Elizabeth. [14]

But indoor social life gave her more opportunity for human relations, and she made the most of it, using every resource for pleasing and winning that she could command. She was the last woman to care for clothes in themselves, but she had all a woman's sense of what they could do for her, properly utilized. When she wanted popularity in Russia, she studied the Russian costume, as she did the Russian language, and made use of both. If there was a great ball on hand, she could outshine everybody in splendor, and again, when others wore their best, she would put on plain garb, and charm the Empress with the fresh simplicity of a country girl.

But her human tact went much deeper than dress. She peered into men's and women's souls, because she could use them and because she was genuinely interested in them. She was a great listener, a great questioner, and people told her all their secrets, because she understood and sympathized. The general testimony to her attraction is too strong to be attributed merely to her great place. To be sure, the ecstasies of Princess Dashkov may require some discounting: 'I really believe there never was any one in the world and certainly never any sovereign who equaled her in the magic versatility of her mind, the exhaustless variety of her resources, and above all the enchantment of her manner, that in itself could give a luster to the commonest words and most trifling matters.' [15] But even Mr. Bernard Shaw, who is not inclined to excessive enthusiasm seems impelled to a conclusion not unlike Princess Dashkov's: 'She not only disputes with Frederick the Great the reputation of being the cleverest monarch in Europe, but may even put in a very plausible claim to be the cleverest and most attractive individual alive.' [16]

Unquestionably a large part of the secret was the fresh, exuberant delight in living which I have already indicated in connection with Catherine's love-affairs. She liked a revel and a frolic, liked to make revel and frolic out of simple things and simple people, liked above all to have others share the frolic with her. She tells fascinating stories in her Memoirs of the freaks and fantasies of her earlier, more irresponsible days in Russia, and up to the very end she describes to Grimm the balls that she attends, one after another. She tells him, a little wistfully, that her grandchildren insist that the wildest game of blindman's buff is not perfect unless grandmother is looking on. Perhaps they really meant it. At any rate, Catherine hoped they did.

III

The greatest frolic of all was being an empress. To appreciate what this meant to Catherine, you have to realize the cramped condition of her German youth, as one can imagine it from reading the Memoirs of the Margravine of Baireuth, the poverty that sent her to Russia with only half a dozen chemises and pairs of stockings, the narrow conventions, the petty formalities, and always the tyranny of small-minded and more or less brutal males. When she came into the new world, she saw how all this might be altered and she determined to alter it.

What she has to say in her Memoirs about her

childish aims and hopes may be in part imagination looking backward. But the burning phrases in her letters to Sir Charles Williams, the English minister who adored her without being her lover, have a magnificent stamp of human truth. After studying so many men and women in all lines who make a pretense of disclaiming the ambition that devours them, it is refreshing to see the complete candor of Catherine's confessions. 'I should tell you that I like to connect everything possible with myself. I thank you for allowing me to do so.' [17] Could there be a more fascinating touch of human nature? Again, see the frankness: 'Two things I know well: one is, that my ambition is as great as is humanly possible; the other, that I shall do some good to your country.' [18] And the ambition is summed up in one admirable phrase, which contains the key to most of Catherine's life: 'Be assured that I shall never play the King of Sweden's easy-going and feeble part, and that I shall either perish or reign.' [19]

Back of the ambition is a quick decision, a tireless persistence, an unshaken courage. It cannot perhaps be maintained that the motto Catherine sets herself would always be adequate, but at least it points the way to great things and sometimes achieves them: 'In my view he who goes ahead is always the one who wins.' [20]

It was in this spirit that she plunged into the complicated tangle that awaited her in Russia. To begin with, she had to deal with the Empress Elizabeth. For years she maneuvered with the most delicate skill, studying the situation in all its aspects, feeling the power of all the intriguing parties, but committing herself to none. Several times she was on the edge of destruction, of being sent back to Germany, of being sent to Siberia, or to heaven. But she weathered it all with consummate tact and judgment.

Then in 1762 the Empress died. Peter succeeded, and in a sense chaos was let loose. It took but a few months to show Catherine that she must either stick to Peter and fall with him, or get rid of him altogether. She did not hesitate. With perfect diplomacy, she connected herself with all those who might hold the power, with the cautious, scheming Panin, with the energetic, executive Orlovs, with minor agents like the enterprising and adventurous Princess Dashkov. Even so, the crisis came before she was really ready. Threatened with discovery of their plots, the Orlovs roused her from her bed one midnight and carried her to the capital with only her maid, her valet, her coiffeur, and a meager attendance. The soldiers flocked to her, first in small groups, then in regiments, and all at once, as if in a dream, she found herself ruler of Russia, with Peter ready to abdicate and begging for tolerance and mercy.

There is something of fantastic, dream quality about the whole of her career. Very soon came the murder of Peter, in which she had no direct hand, but she profited by it. Not long after, the wretched Ivan, grandson of Peter the Great, was also murdered, and again Catherine is exonerated, but again she profited and no one was punished. So for thirty years she maintained herself, appearing to grow stronger and stronger, through all sorts of vicissitudes, malice domestic, as in the dangerous rebellion of Pugachev, in 1774, foreign levy, from Turkey, from Sweden, with cannon thundering almost at her palace gates. She was Duchess of Malfi, Empress of Russia still. Without the slightest hereditary claim, without the smallest traditional preëmption, she kept herself on the throne by sheer force of brains and courage and personal charm.

She enjoyed every year of it, every day of it. She was indeed too intelligent, had too much common sense and too much practical experience of life to set great store by the mere outside of majesty. Yet even here she was a woman and show and parade meant something to her. There was a certain satisfaction in sweeping through her palace halls with all the assumption of dignity and having the rich and the great and the wise bow down to her and acknowledge her sway. There was a real thrill, even up to the end, when she was nearly sixty, in that dreamlike journey which Prince Potemkin staged through the newly conquered Crimea, when the Empress with her suite wandered through dream cities, which had been created, alas, not too substantially, to welcome her, and relished and felt all the breadth and depth of being the sovereign of thirty or forty millions.

There was a more solid satisfaction in the praise and applause of the wisest and greatest men of the age, and this Catherine savored with the keenest zest. She corresponded with her fellow-sovereigns, with Francis Joseph of Austria and Frederick the Great. The letters have little human significance, being mostly a profuse handing out of compliments on both sides, yet when one remembers how Catherine began, her early visit to Frederick's court and humble acceptance of his patronage, there must have been a delicate flavor in being addressed as his royal sister and being deferentially consulted on ways and means for robbing the rest of the world.

Still more agreeable was the correspondence with the intellectual leaders. Voltaire, Grimm, D'Alembert, Diderot, all the great men of France, except Rousseau, wrote to the Empress more or less and they all said nice things to her. The nice things appear to us now a little forced and the flattery a little obvious and artificial. Catherine herself was too shrewd not to see through the artifice at times. She had her moments of rejecting flattery altogether, moments of desperate assertion of the love of truth and sincerity: 'Do you know, it is not praise that does me good, but when men speak ill of me, then, with a noble assurance I say to myself, as I smile at them, "let us be revenged by proving them to be liars."'[21]

Yet the compliments of Voltaires and Diderots are extraordinarily sweet. Those who watched the Empress most closely insisted that her vanity was considerable, as is indeed evident enough from her letters, and that she could be led by flattery if any one chose to take the trouble. She was shrewd, she was sensible, she was practical. When the great issues of life arose, she flung flattery and flatterers from her, and acted as a great sovereign should. But we are all of us more ready to flatter ourselves than any one is to do it for us. The wisest men in the world said she was a great thinker, a great administrator, a great leader, a great empress. After all, they might be right.

Back of the show and the flattery there was the substantial power, the consciousness that the happiness and the misery of millions depended upon your personal autocratic will. To some of us such consciousness would appear to be the height of tragedy, but not when you are constituted as Catherine was. She liked to feel that Europe was swayed by her gracious approval or disapproval. And on the whole it must be admitted that she used her power humanely. Terrible stories are told of the Russian police in her day, as of the Russian police to-day. Police are not comfortable anywhere. Again there is the somewhat doubtful tale of the discarded favorite Mamonov, whose young wife was dragged out of bed for a slight indiscretion and scourged before his eyes. There is undeniable truth in Catherine's own remark: 'I may be kindly, I am ordinarily gentle, but in my line of business I am obliged to will terribly what I will at all.'[22] Yet in her treatment not only of her favorites, but of men and women in general there was a broad, considerate humanity, which was rooted in the deepest and surest foundation, that of being able to put oneself in another's place.

In all this vast appreciation of power and greatness there no doubt were moments of disgust and utter fatigue. What veracity is there in her cry of despair to Grimm: 'In my position you have to read when you want to write and to talk when you would like to read; you have to laugh when you feel like crying; twenty things interfere with twenty others; you have not time for a moment's thought, and nevertheless you have to be constantly ready to act without allowing yourself to feel lassitude, either of body or spirit; ill or well, it makes no difference, everything at once demands that you should attend to it on the spot.' [23]

Sometimes she tried to escape it all, to fly into the country, for simplicity and privacy and rural solitude and peace. She tried to cast off sovereignty, to live with her friends as a simple woman among men and women. She begged them to use the plain thee and thou with her, even to call her Catherine. In her country palace rules were posted for an etiquette which should be no etiquette. Guests were invited to do anything except break the furniture. Fines were imposed upon anybody who forgot himself sufficiently to rise when the Empress came into the room. It was all in vain. As the Prince de Ligne says, they might call her Catherine, but still there was the sense that she was ruler of all the Russias. And she herself complains with a sigh that whenever she comes into a company, it is like introducing the head of Medusa, or again that to be without an equal is simply insupportable.

Yet was it, really? After all, however there might be moments of disgust, there was a singular, enduring relish. And in her advice to the French refugees, written in her latest years, urging them never to give up their hopes of restoration and supremacy, there echoes and resounds the same undying joy in power and greatness that she brought with her to Russia as a girl: 'Reign or die, that is the true device: we should write it on our escutcheon from the very start . . . we must make the world speak of us, we must bear good and bad fortune with an equal glory.'[24]

IV

So, indisputably, she was a great sovereign. Was she also a great ruler? It is at any rate impossible to question her zeal, her ardor, and her indefatigable industry. 'I assure you it is a stern and toilsome business to be what I am,' she writes to Madame Geoffrin.[25] She labors like a shop-girl and wrestles with the great problems of government as if she were a college student struggling for a degree. When she is trying to make over the organization of Russia, she reads vast tomes of law and politics till her eyes and her soul ache. Even the English minister, Harris, who by no means praises her generally, is lost in admiration of her familiarity with Blackstone's Commentaries, and her own enthusiasm over the results of her labors has the winning grace of simple vanity that attaches to so many of her remarks about herself: 'I am undertaking the most foolish work in the world; it is pure madness. The six chapters I have finished are marvels in their kind, each one of them. I am putting into them a labor, an exactitude, a cleverness, and even a touch of genius of which I should not have believed myself capable, and I am overcome with astonishment when a chapter is finished.'[26]

As to the results of her labor there may be a difference of opinion. This is less true of foreign policy than of internal. Her dealings with Europe at large were dominated by one prevailing idea, that of increasing the power and the importance of Russia, as Peter the Great had done. It is true that some critics insist that her methods were inconsistent and erratic. But she herself emphasized her firmness of purpose, and it is probable that her inconsistencies were in the main the opportunism of a great states-man, who adapts his plans to the exigency of the moment. At any rate, the one main aim was never lost sight of.

In the pursuit of it she was perfectly ruthless, and Poland, that country of tragedy, Turkey, Sweden, anybody who got in her way had to take the con-sequences. She was quite as cynical as the great Frederick himself, as appears in his comment on their doings compared with the more scrupulous, or sanctimonious, Empress-Queen of Austria: 'Cath-erine and I,' said Frederick to D'Alembert, 'are two brigands; but that pious Empress-Queen, how does she settle it with her confessor?'[27] And again he puts it still more concisely when he says of Maria Theresa, 'she wept, but she always took.'[28]

What is even more impressive than Catherine's rapacity, which was simply that of ordinary eight-eenth-century politics, is her capacity. You see clearly what this was in the correspondence with Frederick. The great King of Prussia is recognized as the ablest political intelligence of his time, yet the Empress of Russia kept pace with him. He writes to her constantly with the respect and the confidence of an equal and you feel that she is his equal in intellectual grasp as well as in lack of political morality.

And it cannot be denied that from the external point of view Catherine left her empire far greater than she found it, greater in population, greater in wealth, greater in political influence. From her day on Russia has been a factor in European politics that no ruler could afford to overlook or neglect.

With internal affairs the story is not quite so attractive. Here also Catherine's effort was ardent, enthusiastic, and patriotic, but the success was hardly proportionate to the effort. She began her career with the determination to make over the Russian administrative world entirely. Her early letters to Madame Geoffrin and Grimm are full of her zealous studies and her lofty ideal hopes. And there were some aspects in which her labors had permanent and beneficial results. She accomplished much for education, especially in her institute for training girls, which recalls Madame de Maintenon's Saint-Cyr. She organized a most efficient system of administration in the various provinces.

She managed her finances on the whole with extraordinary skill, considering the strain she put upon them by constant war and lavish expenditure.

But her great scheme of constitutional reform in law and administration ended in smoke. After years of labor on it, she submitted it to an Assembly of Notables for discussion and development. The Assembly was quite willing to adulate her and to echo her words, but it was sluggishly indolent, ignorantly unresponsive, and completely overburdened with the age-old weight of Russian traditionalism, and Catherine gave up in disgust.

The crucial point of her failure was serfdom and the condition of the peasants. In the beginning she rebelled against this and urged that it was intolerable. But circumstances were too much for her and at the end of her reign the condition of the serfs was worse than at first. And what happened with serfdom was typical of her larger attitude toward liberalism in general. As a girl she was enraptured by the French philosophers and she began her reign determined to introduce all the blessings of liberty. In theory she cherished the same attitude to the end. But the practice of autocratic rule was not favorable to such ideas. The Pugachev rebellion and similar perils made her draw the reins tighter.

Then all Europe was shaken by the French Revolution, and Catherine, like thousands of other sincere liberals, was horrified into protest. In her later years her letters are full of passionate appeals to the friends of law and order to maintain them against overwhelming ruin.

So the end of her reign has something pathetic, not to say tragic, about it. She seemed to lose her hold, mentally and physically, and especially the flood of financial corruption, always the curse of Russia, affected the government from top to bottom. Yet if you look over Catherine's career as a whole, you cannot fail to recognize grandeur of actual achievement, and still more grandeur of ideal and purpose. She failed in great measure because what she had undertaken was beyond human powers, at any rate beyond the powers of any woman ruler, though few women have more right to the cry of the heroine of the old dramatist:

> Since I can do no good because a woman,
> Reach constantly at something that is near it. [29]

She herself recognized and deplored her feminine limitations. There were times when she sighed to be a man, for, she said, to govern you have to have eyes and hands, and a woman has only ears. More even than a male ruler, she was obliged to depend upon agents and ministers, and her relation to these is one of the most interesting things to study about her. It is urged that she was undiscriminating, did not understand men, and was misled by her passions. That she was sometimes fooled by her passions is undeniable; yet you cannot follow her closely without feeling that she saw through the men she dealt with, even when they fooled her in practice.

In the same way it is urged that all her great actions and political achievements were the work of her ministers, not her own. Here again there appears to be delusion. Like Elizabeth of England, whom she so much resembles, she had a marvelous faculty of identifying herself with clever men, of using, of absorbing, of actually sucking out all the best they had to offer. But she was the final authority and the really dominating force. As Dr. Hötzsch, the judicious analyst of the 'Cambridge Modern History,' puts it: 'Not one of all her many favorites can be said to have ever dominated the Tsarina. Intellectually she was the superior of every one of them and she never allowed her heart to influence her against her better judgment.' [30] No one can read such admirable words as the following and not feel that Catherine was a born ruler

and leader of men: 'In an affair so great as that we
have been speaking of you must be profoundly
penetrated with your object, you must will it passionately, you must then communicate your passion
to others and act accordingly, without hesitating
when your decision is once made, and you must
preserve supreme calm in the midst of all agitation,
never appearing disturbed or anxious about anything that may occur.' [31]

One element of Catherine's success which has
puzzled me a good deal is her hold upon the army.
An autocratic sovereign, in a realm like hers, must
depend largely upon the loyalty of the troops. How
did she secure it? Partly by liberality, but still
more, it appears, by personal appeal and personal
charm. She herself tells us that in the early days of
Peter she used to chat with the sentries and let
them kiss her hand. Later on she used winning and
persuasive words, every sort of patriotic and heroic
urgency that a woman and an empress could use.
And it appears that she succeeded entirely. No
doubt the eulogy of the Prince de Ligne is exaggerated by his personal enthusiasm, but there must
have been much foundation for it. 'It will be remembered that I have seen myself, while journey-
ing two thousand leagues with her through her

dominions, the love and the adoration of her subjects, and in her armies the love and the enthusiasm
of the soldiers. I have seen them in the trenches
braving the balls of the infidels and all the rigor of
the elements, and consoling themselves or animat-
ing their courage with the name of Matouschka,
their mother and their idol.' [32]

The secret of this popularity, however great it
was, the secret of all Catherine's political greatness, of all her achievement, was her devotion to
Russia. From the day she entered the country, she
determined to become Russian, and to rule, if rule
she should, as a Russian and nothing else. She
learned the Russian language till she absolutely
made it her own. She studied Russian history and
Russian thought and Russian life. To say that she
really understood Russia, that vast and complicated
political and social tangle, would be hazardous:
who ever has or does now? To say that she always
worked for its best interests would be more hazardous still. But it is impossible to deny the sincerity
as well as the splendid, solemn ardor of the words in
which she pours out her sense of obligation and
duty to the country which has made her what she is:
'What is certain is that I have never undertaken
anything without being intimately persuaded that

what I was doing was conforming to the good of my Empire; that Empire had done an infinite deal for me; I believed that all my individual faculties, employed constantly for its good, for its prosperity, for its supreme advantage, could hardly suffice to acquit my debt. I have labored to procure the good of every individual everywhere, so far as this did not conflict with the good of the whole.'[33]

V

Now let us get underneath the external achievement and activity to the mental and spiritual constitution of the woman herself. She gives us excellent opportunity to do this, for her correspondence, especially that with Grimm, is as self-revealing as it is extensive.

Take first the æsthetic side, her sense of art, of beauty. She was always a great collector of paintings and her gallery at the Hermitage became one of the wonders of the world. Her letters to Grimm are full of shrewd bargains and large outlay. Now and then she shows real enthusiasm, as in her outburst about the Raphael copies, 'Which have made me cry, pray, scribble all the poor things which it pleases you to call ecstasies and explosions and which sputter all the way from St. Petersburg to

Rome.' [34] But it must be confessed that her enthusiasm is generally more that of the collector than of the lover.

Music meant far less to her than painting. She sometimes enjoys a light opera, but solid concerts bore her: 'I would give anything to hear and to love music, but do the best I can, it is just noise and nothing more.' [35] And with poetry, literature as a fine art, it was little better than with music. She tried in vain to make verses, but never could, perhaps because she had no native language of her own. The theater sometimes stirred her deeply: 'I believed that there was no one who wept as I did over the reading of romances and the representation of tragedies.' [36] She even wrote plays herself, as she wrote a little of everything, from tales to legal disquisitions, and she tells us with naïve joy of the success of her public performances. But the ambition of the author never took hold of her very powerfully.

Nature did not affect her so much as art. One striking element of sensibility in this regard I find in her. In writing to Grimm she several times refers to the impression of great winds, which probably hit her hard, sweeping across the vast spaces of Russia: 'A great wind is blowing, and that gives you either imagination or a headache.' [37] And again, more elaborately: 'It is above all the tempests and the great winds which blow in the morning, when one is fasting, which bring the great strokes of imagination.' [38] But otherwise she does not seem aware of the outward world, except for display. She likes to create gardens and to gather plants, as she gathers pictures. She enjoys country peace and solitude. Nature as a source of emotion means no more to her than to Madame de Maintenon, or Lady Mary Wortley Montagu, or Madame du Deffand. It must be admitted that there was a certain justice in the criticism of Catherine's devoted friend, the Prince de Ligne, 'She had tastes, but no taste.' [39]

In intellectual matters the Empress is far stronger than in æsthetic. She was not perhaps a very profound or a very original thinker, she did not pretend to be so; but she was an enormously and constantly active and energetic one. Her immense correspondence shows how many sides of life she touched, sometimes fleetingly, but always with independence and always with characteristic vigor. She was interested in philosophy, though she admitted her ignorance of it. She was interested in science, theoretically and practically, and herself set the example of inoculation for smallpox. She did what she could to stimulate scientific interest throughout her empire, though the results were not very enduring. She was especially interested in philology and made extensive investigations in Russian and many other languages, which she herself thought highly of, though other authorities are not quite so complimentary. But the point in all the intellectual fields is her superb zeal and her open-mindedness. As she puts it, admirably: 'I am one of the people who love the why of things.' [40] I don't know what more far-reaching scientific motive there can be than that.

And her eager thinking was backed up by constant reading, somewhat indiscriminate, but immensely extensive. In her childhood she read Plutarch and he fed her with great thoughts. She also read various erotic novels, like 'Daphnis and Chloe,' which fed her with other things less desirable. All her life she kept on reading, philosophy, theology, law, politics, especially history, and her reading had a substantial effect upon her action, as her action tempered and solidified her reading, bringing to bear upon it her acute observation of herself and others in a long and varied life. Sometimes the observation inclines to the cynical, as was to be expected: 'I have learned long since to view people as they are, and not as I should wish them to be.' [41] But in general the vast experience leaves her gentle, kindly, tolerant, and certainly not like the melancholy Jaques, 'wrapped in a most humorous sadness.'

In religion the study of Catherine the Great is instructive but not especially edifying. As a child, she was educated in a devout Lutheranism, was surrounded by bigots, as she herself says, and had some spiritual terrors. If so, she got bravely over them. When she went to Russia, she slipped off the Western Church for the Eastern as you would change a pair of gloves, and ever after she maintained the most devout of external religious aspects. On her Crimean journey, whenever she entered a village, she went first to the little church and prostrated herself in prayer, and Masson even tells us that in her private chapel she would throw herself on the floor before the images, gather up the dust from the pavement, and strew it over her crowned head.' [42] Russia was a passionately religious country. She was a Russian Empress and she must do as the Russians did. It was not deliberate hypocrisy. She did not expect any intelligent person to take it seriously. It was political duty, that was all.

Of religious emotion there is not a sign. God, the future life, even death, do not figure in her correspondence, or apparently in her thoughts in any way whatever. You lived while you lived, with all the mad zest that was in you. When you died, you died. That was all there was to it. No college girl of the twentieth century could be more indifferent to the whole matter.

In short, there were two mighty, absorbing elements in her life, and very little else, love and power, surely enough to fill any life, at least pushed to the intensity to which she carried them. The peculiar thing with Catherine, the delightful thing, is that these elements, often tragic and terrible, were so greatly transformed, transfigured by cheerfulness, high spirits, and laughter. She had not perhaps humor in the deepest, dissolving, intellectual sense, the humor of Lincoln or of Lamb. But she had an inexhaustible good nature, an infectious propensity to joy. Voltaire said with justice in regard to her: 'Majesties laugh rarely, though no one needs it more.' [43] Catherine knew how to laugh. As Poniatowski put it, so charmingly, in the early days, 'a soft and pleasant voice and a laugh as merry as her disposition.' [44] The laugh continued to the end, even if sometimes tears quivered in it.

For it was founded on a splendid courage and an indomitable hope.

She loved Sterne, and if she had something of Sterne's artificial eighteenth-century sentimentality, she had also something of his genuine human kindness and of Yorick's undying gayety. Again and again she suggests to me our American Aaron Burr. Her ambition was more fiercely persistent than Burr's. But they both aimed high, they both adored the opposite sex and put little restraint upon their adoration, and they both had a large and most attractive human understanding and gentleness. Perhaps to Burr and certainly to Catherine one cannot do better than apply repeatedly the superb maxim of Ninon, so apt for Ninon herself, 'The joy of a soul is the measure of its force.'

So of the great Empress we may fairly say that, take her for all in all, she was not only great, one of the most energetic, creative, dynamic feminine personalities that ever existed, she was also in many respects thoroughly lovable, and one may even venture to say that she was good, though she was an Empress and she had her little eccentricities.

VI
EVE AND THE PEN
GEORGE SAND

CHRONOLOGY

Amandine Aurore Lucie Dupin Dudevant.
Born, Paris, July 1, 1804.
Lived mainly at Nohant till 1817.
In convent, 1817–1820.
Lived at Nohant till grandmother's death, 1821.
Married M. Dudevant, September 10, 1822.
Began independent life in Paris, January, 1831.
'Indiana' published, 1832.
'Lélia' published, 1833.
Connection with Musset, 1833–1835.
Mother died, 1837.
Connection with Chopin, 1838–1846.
Later quiet life mainly at Nohant.
Died, June 8, 1876.

VI

GEORGE SAND

I

A HUNDRED years ago a young French woman, Amandine Aurore Lucie Dupin, better known as George Sand, tried all the radicalism, all the rebellion, all the emancipations that are supposed to mark the college girl of to-day, and tried them, as Ninon de Lenclos had done two hundred years before, with a thorough fervor and completeness that no college girl of to-day could possibly surpass.

Few persons have had a more picturesque inheritance than Aurore Dupin. Among her ancestors she counted a king of Poland, an opera dancer, and a tenor who sang about the popular concert halls. Born in the climax of the Napoleonic period, in 1804, losing her father when very young, she was brought up in a conflict between her grandmother, who belonged to the old régime, and her mother, who belonged to the new. Yet she had the essentials of strict French education, having been largely trained in a convent. Here she went through an extreme experience of passionate mysticism and then she passed to the other excess of social enjoyment, in both marking characteristic traits of her intensely enthusiastic and intensely human temperament.

After she got out into the world, her mother finally succeeded in bringing about a thoroughly French conventional marriage. Casimir, Baron Dudevant, was a typical country squire, who drank, swore, gambled, and ran after women. He appreciated and respected his wife's superiority and was disposed on the whole to do well by her. But the superiority disconcerted and irritated him. He did not know how to meet it or what to do with it and in the end he found it unendurable.

Aurore at first adapted herself to domestic life with reasonable decorum, and for eight years she continued to be a respectable wife and mother. She bore two children and maternal devotion was at all times one of her most marked characteristics. But gradually her restlessness and discontent grew to be too much for her. Her husband was always indifferent and sometimes brutal. And she came more and more to feel that there were things that she was not getting out of life that she might get and ought to get. In the last of these domestic years there came up a Platonic regard for a certain Aurélien de Sèze, with whom the young wife carried on an ardent correspondence, and when this affair reached a climax and broke off, she felt that the end had come and that she must organize her world on a different basis.

She explained matters to her husband as well as she could, as well as such a situation could be explained, and it must be admitted that on the whole he took it with surprising equanimity. In the end he agreed to give her a modest allowance and to let her spend a portion of every year in complete independence in Paris, while the remainder of the time was to be passed at Nohant in the country with her family.

It was a singular arrangement, but it just suited Aurore. Her life in Paris, when she got there, was perfectly Bohemian. For some years before it had been her practice to ride about her country home in man's costume, and now she bobbed her hair and went through the Paris streets and restaurants in inconspicuous boy's clothing. She smoked cigarettes and cigars like any college girl of to-day and she threw herself into the literary life with all the fervor and all the ardor of creation. At first she had her difficulties. Editors and publishers were reluctant to take her seriously: they could not believe that a young woman from the country could write anything worth while. But she had indomitable courage and persistence, she never gave up. And when she wrote 'Indiana' and 'Valentine' and 'Lélia,' she had the literary world at her feet.

These novels were stories of sex that would enrapture the young woman of the twentieth century, not indeed in the actual tissue of the narrative, since they are long-winded and sentimental and not in the taste or tone that we now prefer; but the substance is the same, the longing of the heart for understanding and sympathy, the vast struggle to realize impossible desires, the tendency to self-expression in all directions.

And if George Sand tried to write sex stories, she was also determined to live them. Not a page of life was to be left unturned, not a savor to be left unrelished. No experiment, however mad, however wild, was to be undared, undone. In the strange phrase in which she puts it to her friend Sainte-Beuve:[1] 'For example, I said to myself: "Is it not permitted to eat human flesh?" You said to yourself: "Perhaps there are persons who ask themselves if it is permitted to eat human flesh." And M. Jouffroy says: "The idea never occurred to any one that human flesh could possibly be eaten."' If such things were to be done, she would do them.

In this spirit she entered upon a long list of experimental lovers. First there was Jules Sandeau, who gave her half of his name, and wrote her early novels with her, and deceived her, and undeceived her, or so she thought. And there was Mérimée, for a little time, who seemed as hopelessly unsuited to her as a human being could be. And there was the long romance with Alfred de Musset, which came near to wrecking both their lives. There was the passionate idyl at Fontainebleau and the disillusion in Venice, which both of them told over in strange, high-wrought narratives afterwards. And in the midst of this Venetian ecstasy George went astray with the Italian doctor Pagello.

After she returned home, the advocate who was defending her cause and helping her to get a final separation from her husband for the time established an ascendency over her, until his control became too urgent and too annoying. And this infatuation yielded at length to the influence and presence of Chopin, who for eight years was an inmate of George's household, traveled with her, worked with her, suffered and enjoyed with her, and mingled her life so much with the tissue of his own that it seemed as if they could never be torn apart.

And all the time and until her death in 1876, she was writing life as well as living it, turning her own passionate experience into more passionate stories for others. And all the time she was living a home life as a mother and even as a wife, for after all she was an essentially domestic creature, and home habits and home thoughts and home preoccupations were essential to her, and she sometimes said that there was nothing in the world she cared so much for as she did for her children, and perhaps she was right.

II

Through all these mad adventures and strange experiences the distinguishing feature and the fundamental characteristic of George Sand's temperament was her essential idealism. And I ask myself whether in this she differs from the young person of the present day, whether the cynical after-wisdom of the Great War has really destroyed the illusions of youth, or whether there is still beneath the cynicism the undying aspiration and the unconquerable hope. Certainly these things were present in George Sand always, and always she retained an extraordinary, persistent power of self-delusion about persons and things. The remarkable point is that, especially in earlier years, the delusion was accompanied by the most piercing bursts and flashes of clear vision, of cynical disillusion, when for the moment all the bare ugliness of fact and truth stood out in its prevailing horror. No one could appreciate this horror or state it more clearly or violently, for the time, than she did. Then the ideal dream again involved the world, and men and women and life were once more enveloped in a mist of tenderness and love and charm. As one who knew her well and had long lived with her passionately expressed it: 'To live beside Madame Sand was to live in a world of beautiful chimæras, of charming utopias, of limitless dreams.' [2] Or, in her own engaging phrase: 'I know nothing in the world but loving and believing in an ideal.' [3] Yet the strange mixture of disillusion with the illusion shows well in a bitter passage of a letter written when she was thirty years old: 'I would be cut in pieces for ideas that will never be realized in my lifetime. I would render service to the lowest of creatures for the hopes of my whole life, which perhaps has been nothing but one long dream. Yet if I followed my instincts, I should not pull my neighbor's child out of the water. Therefore there is something in me that would be odious, if it were not simple infirmity, the mere remnant of a malady that has been acute.' 4

The most striking illustration of George Sand's idealism is her Autobiography, the 'Histoire de Ma Vie.' Here everything is in a sense veracious. There is truth of detail, undeniable record of indisputable fact. Yet somehow, over everything, there is a sweet, sunlit glow, a pervading atmosphere of gentle tenderness, which transforms and transfigures, gives a touch of unreality, or more properly of ideality, to the most unpromising incidents and the most unattractive people.

We get this effect at the very threshold with the elaborate studies of the grandmother and the mother. Both these women are suggested and portrayed as they really were, no doubt, at moments almost remorselessly. Yet something in the perspective, something in the grace of touch, something in the handling of the accessories makes us see them with the charm and the attraction that they both had for the daughter and the granddaughter, with the real devotion that she undoubtedly felt for both of them, different as they were.

If George Sand was a thoroughgoing idealist as a daughter and granddaughter, she was equally so as a mother. She worshiped her son Maurice from his cradle with adoration and admiration, but he only moderately justified the feelings. He had a touch of his mother's genius, but he was an amateur, where she was always professional. Maurice was an amateur novelist. He was an amateur botanist and scientist. He was an adept in amateur theatricals and kept the house at Nohant in a flurry with the noise and bustle of his constant dramatic performances. But he was by no means ever the genius that his mother thought he was.

With Solange, the daughter, the case was different. Solange, as so often happens, was too like her mother for the two to get on comfortably together. She ran much the same career that her mother did, but she had not the illusions, and to the mother the illusions were the essence of life. George did her best, but she complains in despair of how little she accomplished: 'I brought her into the world, I cherished her, whipped her, adored her, spoiled her, scolded her, punished her, pardoned her, and with it all I do not understand her in the least.' [5] And she breaks out into the old, old cry that the girl belongs to another generation: 'This age is accursed and she is the child of the age: there is no religion in her soul.' [6] Which is exactly the sort of thing that the older generation said of George herself.

Solange quarreled with Maurice because of a young woman, whom the mother rather unwisely introduced into the family. The daughter married a brute, against her mother's wishes, left him, and began the same irregular life that her mother had lived, to her mother's infinite disgust. Maurice quarreled with the son-in-law so violently that George was at length obliged to forbid him the house, and she even warns Maurice not to eat in his sister's home for fear they should attempt to poison him.[7] Yet with it all she did what she could to keep on good terms with Solange to the end, and the death of Solange's little daughter Jeanne was one of the cruelest blows the grandmother ever had to meet.

And George Sand was an idealist in larger human relations as well as in the more personal. She had a genius for friendship and the supreme gift of see-ing and cherishing what was best in those she loved. In general society she was neither easy nor responsive. Heine, in his elaborate account of his early acquaintance with her, insists that she was shy and quiet, not a talker but a listener,[8] and the Goncourts give very strongly the same impression.

GEORGE SAND

She was not especially beautiful, small and almost insignificant when you first met her, but what every one emphasizes is the searching power and penetrating effect of her dark eyes. 'All her intelligence seemed to have withdrawn into her eyes, abandoning the rest of her countenance to the material,' says Tocqueville,[9] and most of those who describe her seem to have felt the eyes as distinctly predominant. She had little wit, little laughter herself, though she had a strange vein of nonsense which appears in some of the early letters to Flaubert and elsewhere. She liked to have a whirlwind of gayety about her and the house at Nohant was often alive with practical jokes and a robust sort of fooling, which delighted Maurice but was sometimes rather disconcerting to casual visitors. The hostess herself, however, took little part in all this, but moved through it, indifferent, quiet, evasive, absorbed in her own thoughts and dreams.

The climax, the fine flower, the full embodiment of George Sand's ideal instinct and genius for friendship, appear in the correspondence between her and Flaubert, which, like those between Goethe and Schiller, or between Emerson and Carlyle, is one of the great spiritual exchanges of the world, and is perhaps the most remarkable.

What is striking is the complete difference of the two correspondents. Flaubert, in theory at any rate, was the least idealistic of men, cold-blooded, keen-sighted, cynical, realistic in his mental attitude. George Sand was visionary, imaginative, a weaver of dreams. Yet by sheer breadth of character and loftiness of spiritual purpose and level, they were able to understand, to respect, to enjoy, and to love each other. And what is further notable is the way in which George Sand secures and maintains her spiritual superiority. Able and noble as Flaubert was, you feel in her the larger and the loftier nature, and, as with Emerson and Carlyle, you are all the time aware, in Emerson's own phrase, that George Sand is 'writing down to Flaubert' and that he realizes and instinctively acknowledges her supremacy.

But the chief manifestation of George Sand's idealism was undoubtedly in her love affairs, and it is here above all that her vast effort to realize the impossible finds its scope and its full play. She was determined to distill the last drop, the last atom of celestial rapture that love would yield her and she made upon poor human nature demands more severe than it could possibly satisfy. She wanted love to develop every aspect and phase of emotion. As she herself put it: 'I have known many kinds of love. The love of the artist, the love of the woman, the love of the sister, the love of the mother, the man's love, the poet's love — I know not what.' [10] The mother-instinct, especially, was marked in her, and, again in her own words, 'my dominant passion, as you say, has been maternity. In all the sentiments, all the loves of my life, there has been something of the protecting passion which causes us to feel that those whom one loves peculiarly belong to one.' [11] This makes her an excellent mark for the comment of the Freudians, and the Œdipus theory has in her one of its most luminous illustrations. Indeed, both she and Musset note, with a sort of shrinking horror, a maternal element in their caresses and they both mark it as almost approaching incest.

In consequence of this maternal and protecting quality, it has been suggested and asserted that the mere passion of the senses was a lesser feature in George Sand's love-making than the imagination and that in this aspect she was not a lover of the most violent order. But there seems to me to be a misunderstanding here, so far as one can judge on such a point, and I believe that she was as capable of passion as any woman could be. The distinction in her case was that she had in a high degree the feminine reluctance to accept the flesh without the spirit, she was passionately bound to infuse the ardor of the spirit into the last intensity of physical rapture. It is with this that Flaubert reproaches her in his outcry, too gross for English words, 'women who mistake their senses for their heart,' and her attitude is well summed up in the lines of the old poet D'Avenant,

> Fond maids, who love with mind's stuff would mend,
> Which Nature purposely of bodies wrought. [12]

But George Sand has expressed the same thing most vividly and effectively in the letter of astonishingly frank self-confession which she wrote to Grzymala as a prelude to accepting Chopin as a lover. In regard to physical love she says: 'This way of looking at the last embrace of love has always been repugnant to me. If the last embrace is not as sacred, as pure, as devoted as the rest, there is no virtue in abstaining from it.... Can there be for lofty natures a purely physical love and for sincere natures a purely intellectual one?... To *distrust the flesh* cannot be good and useful except for those who are *all flesh*.... The magnet embraces the iron, the animals come together by the difference of sex.... Man alone regards this miracle which takes place

simultaneously in his soul and his body as a miserable necessity, and he speaks of it with distrust,
with irony, or with shame. This is passing strange.
The result of this fashion of separating the spirit
from the flesh is that it has necessitated convents
and brothels.' [13] Always the cry of the incurable
idealist, and one recurs to D'Avenant,

> Which Nature purposely of bodies wrought.

With such an attitude towards the possibilities
and the satisfactions of love, it is obvious that
George Sand would not be likely to find much contentment in lovers of flesh and blood. She did not.
She tried one after another, demanded of all of
them raptures and ecstasies and perfection that
human nature could not give, and the result was
disillusion and disaster: 'Is a lofty and believing
love a possible thing? Must I die without ever
having met with it? Always to be clasping phan-
toms and pursuing shadows — I am weary of it.' [14]
And still, still she insisted that she was constant,
faithful to her ideal at any rate: 'Thus far I have
been faithful to what I have loved, absolutely
faithful in the sense that I have never deceived any
one, and that I have never been unfaithful without
very strong reasons, which by the fault of others

have killed the love in me. I am not inconstant by nature.' [15]

In the search for the fulfillment of her ideal she turned first to one typical aspect of it and then to another. Musset, for example, the frail, delicate, high-wrought, sensitive, poetical child, brought out all the maternal instinct in her. Her first thought with him was care and fostering tenderness and motherly solicitude. For a long time they clung to each other with desperate passion. Life apart seemed absolutely impossible, and the alternative of death together was to be preferred and sought: 'All this, you see, is a game that we are playing; but our hearts and our lives are the stakes, and things are not quite so gay as they appear to be. Shall we go blow out our brains together at Franchart? It will be the quickest and easiest way.' [16] And they did not blow out their brains, and they parted, and they felt that they could not live apart and came together again, and they parted once more for good and all.

Then there was the strange interlude of the Venetian doctor, Pagello, to whom the lady offered herself, apparently because he embodied an ideal of sanity and health and robust common sense and everything that the frail and nervous poet had not.

And here again there was disappointment, for muscle and common sense were no more satisfying in the end than imagination and nerves.

And the next resource was the radical and political advocate, who represented brains. Perhaps after all brains were a surer comfort, a more adequate source of companionship, than either nerves or muscles. But the brains failed also, proved in the end hard and dry and exacting, even more difficult to live with comfortably than the muscles or the nerves.

So the poor lady once more resorted to the fundamental instinct of mother and nurse and took on her hands the invalid Chopin, and kept him for eight years, more as a tenderly fostered and protected child than as a lover. Yet all the time she resented the lack of love, and the terrible, furious exchange of passion, which was just as necessary to her as the fostering tenderness. And in the end she wearied of being nurse and mother, wearied finally of the hopeless attempt to be lover at all, and settled down, with age and satiety, to the gray and dreary acceptance of a life in which love was an admitted impossibility and the ideal must remain for ever unrealized.

But through all this wide, long Odyssey of

amorous quest, what is notable is the singular ideal
candor of her spiritual attitude. Never once does
the notion of offense or sinning occur to her. Her
aim throughout has been of the highest, her intention has been pure. Of what account is it that her
action has sometimes faltered and gone astray?
How delightful is her description of herself as
'*presque vierge*,' or as our slang of to-day would
have it, 'a near-virgin.' [17] There is no sense of soil
or stain about her, no admission of wrongdoing in
any way whatever. The perpetual cry of her
heroines and herself, the Valentines, the Indianas,
the Lélias, is that life is imperfect and inadequate
and incomplete, not they. 'I admit to you that the
desire to fit any philosophy at all to my own sentiments has been the great preoccupation and the
great pain of my life. My sentiments have always
been stronger than reason and the limits I have
wanted to set for myself have ever been useless. I
have changed my ideas twenty times. Above everything I have believed in fidelity. I have preached
it, practiced it, demanded it. It has failed, and so
have I. And yet I have felt no remorse, because in
my infidelities I have always submitted to a kind
of fatality, an instinct for the ideal which pushed
me into leaving the imperfect for what seemed to

me to be nearer to the perfect.' [18] It is the same eternal cry of the unsatisfied idealist, the demand for the impossible, the perpetual aspiration and the perpetual disillusion that inevitably accompanies it. And no better words can be found for it than the passionate utterance of Lélia herself: 'Love, Sténio, is not what you think; it is not the violent bending of all the faculties towards a created being, it is the sacred aspiration of the most ethereal portion of our soul toward the unknown. Creatures bound down by impassable limits, we ceaselessly seek to delude the insatiable desires that consume us; we strive to find them an object near at hand, and poor prodigals that we are, we endow our perishable idols with all the immaterial beauty that adorns our dreams. The emotions of the senses do not suffice us. Nature has nothing perfect enough in all its treasure-house of naïve joys to appease the thirst for happiness that is within us: we require heaven, and we have it not.' [19]

III

As George Sand was an idealist in concrete human relations, so it would naturally be expected that she would be an idealist in her chosen profession of novel-writing. She was an idealist in the general conception and handling of her work and in the method and detail of it. Long and laborious planning to carry out elaborately conceived intellectual effort was not her way. Everything was inborn, instinctive, spontaneous. From her childhood she was a weaver of dreams, and when she determined to write, all she had to do was to weave her dreams and reveries into tangible human relations. Her childish invention of the peculiar god Corambé, for her personal worship, was typical, and like the youthful Goethe, she framed a woodland altar for her own special god. Like Sir Walter Scott, she was always accustomed to put together fantastic tales, purely for her own amusement and diversion, long before she ever thought of setting them down in cold print for the diversion of the whole world. As she herself expresses it, broadly and generally: 'Literature must be the teaching, direct or indirect, of the ideal.' [20]

And as her conceptions were instinctive and spontaneous, her method of production was equally so. Nothing brings out more clearly than this the contrast between her and her friend Flaubert. Flaubert toiled over his sentences and put his phrases together with agonized pains. He could not work at all except in silence and solitude, with ab-

solute freedom from distraction and interruption.
George Sand could drop down and write anywhere.
She had paper and pens all over the house, so that
she could catch her thoughts whenever they overcame her. She could write with the children playing about her and the parrot chattering. She would
not have set hours, or ordered plans, or definite,
systematic production of any kind. All was inspiration. Her art came to her and she took it just
as it came. Her work undeniably had the defects of
improvisation. It was often slovenly, heedless,
and incomplete, unfinished. But it had the charm of
improvisation also, the wide, sure sweep, the divine, natural ease, the unfailing, instinctive grace
of movement. All these things Flaubert saw and
envied, saw and wondered how she achieved at a
touch the easy perfection which he toiled so long
and so vainly to attain. With George Sand to
write was as natural as to breathe and it is quite
credible that the stories flowed so easily that she
could finish one after midnight and begin another
before morning.

Again, the idealistic attitude shows in the treatment of ambition, the long and eager quest for distinction and glory. No one felt the enthusiasm of
her art more than George Sand did, her art which

she 'loved more than anything else in the world.'
The excitement and the passion of creation meant
everything to her. But just because it was all inborn, there was little conscious effort about it.
She did not deliberately seek success because of the
popularity and glory that went with them. She
wrote because it was natural to her and she could
not help it. It was her form of expressing the deepest needs and passions of her spirit. They were in
her and they had to come out. As she puts it to
Flaubert: 'There is no being who has more calm and
inward happiness than this aged troubadour, withdrawn from the tumult of the world, who sings
from time to time his little romance to the moon,
with very little care whether he sings well or ill,
provided he can get out the melody which is running in his head.' [21] This was in age, but in the
early days the note was much the same: 'As I have
no ambition to be known, I never shall be. The
greater part of writers live in bitterness and
struggle, I know; but those who have no greater
ambition than to earn their livelihood live in the
shadow peaceably.' [22] And no doubt many authors
make these disclaimers of ambition and in most
cases one suspects either self-deception or deliberate
hypocrisy under such statements. But they seem

to come as near being true with George Sand as with any one.

There is the idealistic attitude again in regard to money. Personally George Sand's needs and her habits were simple. She was indifferent to luxury and required for herself only the bare necessities of life. Under the commercial and bourgeois régime which she hated it seemed to her that wealth always meant dishonesty: 'In a society such as ours is can one respect the delicacy of sentiment and do what is called business? No! Honest people are condemned to be beggars.' [23]

Also, George Sand was always honorably scrupulous in money matters. An obligation was an annoyance to her and a debt was quite intolerable. As she writes to Buloz, her favorite editor: 'You know, that a debt frets me like a sore.' [24] It worried her when she got behindhand. It distressed her to have her affairs out of order and to feel that she had undertaken financial responsibilities that she could not meet.

On the other hand, with money, as with other things, order and system were repugnant to her. Routine she hated, and for most of us in money matters routine is the only safety. And she was at all times an immense and constant spender. It was not her own personal needs that consumed the money. It was the needs and demands of those about her, and her generosity was unlimited. 'I can go without things myself,' she says, 'even without what appear to be necessities; but I cannot bear that a cat among those about me should feel the effects of this.' [25]

Consequently she was too often short of cash and had to get it as best she could, and the result was not always advantageous to her art. The painter Delacroix, who knew her well and observed her carefully, bewails this, and complains that money-getting was almost as disastrous to her as to her contemporary Dumas: 'The necessity of writing at so much a page is the dismal cause that would undermine even more robust talents. They turn the volumes that they pile up into money and under such conditions masterpieces become impossible.' [26] Not impossible certainly, but much more difficult, and too many of George Sand's chapters, if not books, showed a tendency to become pot-boilers under the unfortunate influence of financial pressure.

With the passage of years the money did flow in, and with it came glory and popular applause. And it would be idle to deny that George Sand enjoyed

these things, however she might disclaim them and
announce her indifference to them. 'The artist
works to live,' she may cry, 'and I more than any
other; for I care nothing for glory and I have huge
need for money.' [27] But when men praised her, she
liked it, and above all, when they neglected her and
grew indifferent and turned to other work and other
workers, she felt the sting. There is no field of the
artist's effort where these successes and failures are
appreciated more immediately or more tangibly
than in the theater, and for many years George
Sand worked at the theater, with varying fortune
and with infinite satisfaction as well as disappointment. It is impossible not to share the spontaneous
delight which thrills through an account like the
following: 'The success grew with every act. In
short, it was all that can be imagined of spontaneous and genuine triumph. There were no political
allusions, no outside preoccupations whatever.
Everybody was absorbed in the play and the emotion of it. They laughed, they wept, and all sorts
of effects came out that nobody anticipated.' [28] Or
again, there is the description of the performance
of 'Le Marquis de Villemer': 'The theater was
crowded, overflowing; the tirade of Ribes, in the
second act, provoked simple delirium.... The actors

were recalled after every act. They could hardly finish the play. The applause made them literally intoxicated. Berton is still drunk with it this morning, though his usual drink is nothing but reddened water. All the evening he followed me through the wings, telling me that he owed me the greatest success of his life and the finest rôle that he had ever played.' [29]

You may preserve a singular apparent stoicism through such scenes as this: 'If you had seen how calm I was through it all, you would have laughed; for I was no more moved with fear or with pleasure than if it had not affected me personally at all and I cannot tell you why.' [30] But such moments do not come too often in any one's life and there are few who do not remember them with ecstasy afterwards.

If George Sand was an idealist in artistic method and attitude, she was quite as much so in artistic achievement. Not for her was the slow, laborious rendering of the sordid detail of the surface of life, but there was always the impetuous effort to transfigure reality with ideal beauty. Sometimes this was accomplished by artistic climaxes, and when these grew naturally and logically out of the movement and development of the story, they were often in a high degree impressive and effective, as with the admirable theatrical triumphs of Consuelo, which it is impossible for any sympathetic reader to resist. And again there was deference to the cheap romantic devices of the day, the hidden trapdoors, the mysterious caverns, the tricks and passwords, which make the later portion of this same 'Consuelo' rather wearisome to the modern reader. Even in the best of her novels George Sand was too much inclined to claptrap of this sort, in the vein of 'The Castle of Otranto' and Mrs. Radcliffe.

The same idealism of handling appears in the region of character. This was never George Sand's strong point, and her range and variety of human types is comparatively limited. For women it may well be said that the only figure she drew with real power and success was herself. There is always a contrasted type, for purposes of conflict and comparison, the Anaïs of 'Valentine,' the Pulchérie of 'Lélia,' the Amélie of 'Consuelo.' But in all the novels the same heroine appears, strong, modest, self-contained, unpretentious but dominant and dominating, Valentine, Indiana, Consuelo, the Thérèse of 'Elle et Lui,' Lucrezia Floriani, above all, Lélia, and always this heroine is George Sand.

It is curious to see how the same personage is manifest in the autobiography, 'Histoire de Ma Vie,' and always with the leading position, the *beau rôle*. The extraordinary thing is that this figure should be so dominant and so charming, and every one of these heroines commends herself with a winning magic that is difficult to understand.

It is far otherwise with the heroes. It is indeed humiliating to the human male to feel that women so shrewd, so keen-sighted, and so different as Jane Austen and George Sand should misunderstand and misinterpret him so completely—if only they did not understand him too well. The men of George Sand fall into two distinct types. There is the spoiled, high-strung, over-sensitive child, who is chiefly embodied in Alfred de Musset, the Bénédicts, the Sténios, man as George Sand really saw him, a creature to be petted and nursed and fostered and despised. And there is the hero whom she would have liked to see, the Trenmor of 'Lélia,' Albert in 'Consuelo,' who combines the passions of the man with the intellect of the god. And under it all you cannot help feeling a vast instinctive contempt, a sense that the sole function of the male is to fecundate the female and then die. Now masculine vanity does not wholly relish such a view of the end and aim of the male human being in the universe.

It is curious to reflect that this conception of the great feminine idealist finds its counterpart, to a large extent, in the treatment of the world's great realistic artist, Shakespeare. The men of Shakespeare certainly appear — to other men — more real than those of George Sand, but their reality is to the full as earthy as that of her men. And Shakespeare's women have the same ideal superiority, the Portias, the Violas, the Imogens, have all the celestial, sustained perfection that belongs to Lélia and Consuelo.

But undoubtedly what most idealizes these various elements in George Sand is the charm and the magic of her style. It is not in all ways a perfect style. It is too facile, too flowing, at times almost approaching the slipshod. But its very quality of inprovisation gives it a divine ease and grace which all the long labor of Flaubert could never equal. There is a depth and a delicacy of rhythm, which no translation can suggest, but which is hardly surpassed in any French prose anywhere. And it is interesting to find George Sand herself emphasizing the point of rhythm and especially insisting upon her effort to establish and maintain it. She writes to her daughter: 'In general one should study in the construction of phrases what is called *number* ... my frequent erasures, which you will do well to examine, all tend to reëstablish a certain equilibrium where it is lacking and to diminish it where there is an appearance of excess.' [31] It is this echoing, penetrating rhythmic quality that Thackeray suggested when he said that George Sand's diction 'recalled the sound of country bells falling sweetly and sadly on the ear.' [32]

The most enduring element of beauty in George Sand, the source of unfailing delight, is her description of the natural world. Here she had not only poetic idealism, but a secure basis of exact and scientific observation, since she was an ardent botanist and geologist. And the strength and depth of her nature feeling lies in her sense of the simple everyday things that are about us everywhere. She often felt and described striking scenes and exceptional situations. But she was most at home in the quiet rural landscape with which she had grown up and her best novels are full of this landscape, 'Valentine' and the pastoral stories, 'La Petite Fadette,' 'François Le Champi,' which are perhaps her most permanent work. In all these there is the feeling of open fields and clear sky, of winding woodpaths traced through the witchery of sinuous green, of delicate ferns and fading flowers, scattered in exhaustless profusion over the nuptials of lovers and their burial places.

And after the gorgeous luxury of summer days, there is the serene majesty of winter nights, and the tranquil splendor of the stars. Perhaps no writer has rendered this high-wrought glory of night with more largeness or more intensity than George Sand, as for example in the invocation to Sirius, in 'Lélia': 'Sirius, king of the long nights, sun of the somber winter, thou that precedest the dawn in autumn and plungest beneath our horizon in quest of the sun of spring! Brother of the sun, Sirius, monarch of the firmament, thou who bravest the white clarity of the moon when all the other stars pale before her, and who piercest with eye of fire the heavy veil of misty nights. O the fairest, O the grandest, the most brilliant of the torches of the night, pour down thy white rays upon my dewy locks, restore hope to my trembling soul and vigor to my frozen limbs. Shine about my head, illuminate my way, pour upon me the waves of thy rich light. King of the night, guide me to the beloved of my heart!' [33]

IV

As the final phase of George Sand's idealism, we should consider its interpenetration of her intellectual and spiritual life.

She was a thoroughgoing idealist in politics and threw herself with whole-hearted ardor into all the democratic enthusiasm of her time. The revolution of 1848 inspired her with all the hopes, all the vague aspirations that it brought to so many eager lovers of humanity, and when it failed and passed in the imperialism of Napoleon Third, the disappointment was as crushing for her as for others, though her ardent power of hoping reconciled her to the new régime more speedily than others were able to accomplish it.

Sainte-Beuve reproaches George Sand with her readiness to accept political ideas second-hand from others, and it is true that she was quick to catch new theories and was a ready and responsive follower of Saint-Simonism, and of the notions of Le Roux, of Mazzini, and of many other political agitators. What Sainte-Beuve misses is the human intensity and the inborn fervor of instinctive idealism, which enabled George Sand to take the theories of others into her spirit and make them her own with a new significance and a far-reaching vitality.

These qualities of human love and sympathy were precisely what Sainte-Beuve lacked, and the abundance of them is what makes George Sand eternally lovable and great. It is her undying belief in human nature and her unbounded love for it, even when she does not and cannot believe in it, that will always appeal in her. Love was the essential principle of her life, love for individuals, love for mankind in general, a spontaneous outflow of maternal tenderness, as inexhaustible as it is delightful. Back of her political optimism was an unconquerable belief in the future, as in the admirable sentence that Matthew Arnold quotes from her: 'Our ideal life, which is no other than our normal life as we are called upon to live it.' [34] Or again, 'The ideal, the dream of my social conception, is in the sentiments that I find in myself, but that I could never force by demonstration into hearts not open to such sentiments.' [35] And she expounds the same ideas to Flaubert with even more intensity of passionate ardor: 'I pity humanity, I want it to be good, because I cannot separate myself from it, because it is myself, because the evil that it does cuts me to the heart, because its shame makes me blush, because its crimes wring my soul, because I cannot conceive of paradise either in earth or heaven for myself alone.' [36]

DAUGHTERS OF EVE

The distinguishing feature of George Sand's intellectual life was an incessant, restless, unappeasable mental activity. Her thinking may not have been always original or profound, but it was manifold and unceasing as that of Catherine the Great. In the preface to 'Lélia' she speaks of 'the anguish which is inexplicable to those who live without seeking the cause and the end of life.' She was not one of them: life to her was a matter of questions and problems and she was agonized by the ceaseless endeavor to solve the problems and answer the questions. Even in her childhood she ran over a vast collection of French and English and German philosophers, and the result was a jumble of theorizing from which she never altogether escaped.

The first phase of this spiritual effort was an application of her uncompromising ideal standards to the actual facts of life with disastrous consequences. Compared with the dream of what the world should be, the realization of what it actually was was hideous, disgusting, unthinkable, and she fell into a despairing pessimism, from which the only refuge was passionate rebellion, the determination to do everything that in her lay to make the world different and more like the ideal that she had always dreamed. Nowhere are there finer, more inspiring utterances of this Promethean attitude,

> The courage never to submit or yield,
> And what is else not to be overcome,

than in some of the pages of 'Lélia.'

The inevitable outcome of such disgust with this world was the thought of leaving it. From a very early age the idea of suicide seems to have been a familiar one and death was prefigured not as something horrible, but as a sweet possible refuge, an always open door of escape. 'Oh, enlighten me, infinite light. Why hast thou permitted that from my tenderest age death has always appeared to me so beautiful and so attractive?' [37] Not only in the tragic climaxes of her love-affairs, but at many other periods, this thought of suicide intrudes and recurs.

But such an attitude cannot continue: it must terminate in disaster or change. The two alternatives appear to be, either to get out of life finally and completely or to accept it as it is. And with the passage of years George Sand compels herself to such acceptance and makes it ample and entire. The transition by which this is effected is the transference of emphasis from self to others. Not to live in the meager, circumscribed I, but in the larger,

ampler unity of all things, that is the transforming
secret! 'This feeling that *the whole* is greater, nobler,
stronger, and better than we, keeps us in the lovely
dream that you call the illusions of youth and that
I for my part call the ideal, that is the view and the
sense of what is true above the circle of the nar-
rower horizon. I am an optimist in spite of all that
has torn me to pieces, it is perhaps the sole great
quality that I have.' [38]

This sense of the whole takes the more definite
and concrete form of a growing belief in God. Even
in earlier days Lélia had been haunted by a mystical
preoccupation with the divine; but as time went
on, this vague instinct of spiritual communion
crystallized to an increasing confidence in a more
tangible deity, something analogous to the *Dieu
des bons gens* of Béranger, a tolerant, amiable,
creating, sustaining father, who is patient with
the waywardness of his creatures because he is responsible for it. And with this belief in God goes a
steady belief in a future life and an assurance that
we shall once more, somewhere, somehow, see and
converse and live with those we love. This belief is
insisted upon frankly because life is felt to be impossible without it.

For it must be admitted that, charming and attractive as this later spiritual phase of George Sand is, there is a certain unreality in it which detracts something from its value. She herself, with the magnificent candor and clear-sightedness which are among her chief charms, was ready to the end to admit the forced and artificial quality of her optimistic attitude. Such an admission peeps out in her saying to Flaubert, in her very last years: 'I cannot forget that my personal victory over despair has been the work of my will and of a new fashion of looking at life, altogether opposed to that I used to have.' [39] At an earlier period, when the change was taking place, she emphasizes the same thing: 'Although it would be better *poetically* to absorb Sténio in Lélia than Lélia in Sténio, I think that *as a matter of fact* the contrary is preferable. It is wiser to become credulous through happiness than to persist in scepticism while avoiding the delights that overcome it.' [40] There were moments when the rosy veil of idealism was split and torn apart, when she became bitterly aware of the hollowness and emptiness of a life lived wholly for others, and a black gulf of doubt and death opened yawning beneath her feet. Such a moment is suggested in the passage of another late letter to Flaubert: 'How you torment yourself and how you

allow life to overcome you! For what you complain
of is life: it has never been better for any one or in
any age. We feel it more or less, we understand it
more or less, we suffer from it more or less, and the
more one is in the advance of the age in which one
lives, the more one suffers. We pass like shadows
on a background of clouds, which the sun hardly
and rarely pierces, and we cry unceasingly for
this sun which cannot be had. It is our business to
clear away the clouds as best we can.'[41] Then the
rosy veil knits together again, she reaffirms her
would-be tranquil assurance of God and of the future, and forgets.

It is because of this element of unreality in her
optimistic attitude that, at any rate to those who
do not perfectly sympathize with that attitude, the
real, the immortal George Sand will remain the poet
of an earlier day, the Lélia whom she so often declared to be identified with herself, the spirit of
eternal longing, eternal question, eternal despair.
It is the magnificent rebel who demanded of existence the impossible, which it could never yield,
who at all times asked too much of life, who was
passionately set upon making the world over on
an ideal model, who looked and longed for 'the
ideal life, which is none other than the normal life

as we are called to know it.' And no utterance of
hers will endure longer or echo more supremely in
the ear of mankind than the outcry of Lélia on
the platform of Camaldoli: 'I grope in darkness and
my tired arms grasp nothing save delusive shadows.
And for ten thousand years, as the sole answer to
my cries, as the sole comfort in my wretchedness, I
hear astir, over this earth accurst, the despairing
sob of unrelieved agony. For ten thousand years I
have cried in infinite space: *Truth! Truth!* For ten
thousand years infinite space keeps answering me:
Desire! Desire! O Sibyl forsaken! O mute Pythia!
dash then thy head against the rocks of thy cavern,
and mingle thy raging blood with the foam of the
sea; for thou deemest thyself to have possessed the
Almighty Word, and these ten thousand years thou
art seeking him in vain.' [42] Such an outcry may be
tragic, hopeless, despairing, terrible; it is at least
real, and there is a vast depth of human nature
under it.

VII
EVE IN THE SPOTLIGHT
SARAH BERNHARDT

CHRONOLOGY

Born, Paris, October 23, 1844.
Entered the Conservatoire, 1860.
Played 'Iphigénie' at Théâtre Français, 1862.
Returned to the Français, 1872.
Left the Français and toured America, 1880.
Married Damala, 1882.
Took Porte Saint-Martin, 1883.
Husband died, 1889.
In America, 1891–1893.
Took Renaissance, 1893.
In America, 1896.
Théâtre Bernhardt established, 1899.
Lost leg, 1915.
Died, March 26, 1923.

VII

SARAH BERNHARDT

I

SARAH BERNHARDT's superbly characteristic motto was, *Quand même* — Even if — What if it does — No matter. Take the sweet of life, crowd it full of beauty and splendor, make a tumultuous riot and revel of it. No matter if disasters come, and diseases, and decay, no matter if crooked fortune does her spitefulest, you will have had your hour and made the most of it — *Quand même*.

Assuredly no career could be more startling or more picturesque. Born in Paris, in 1844, of dubious paternity, Jewish in origin, Catholic and conventual in training, sometimes fondled and petted by her mother, sometimes neglected and abandoned for months together, the child was finally flung into the whirlpool of the Parisian theater. For years she struggled perilously, escaping disaster by miracle, but her genius and her magnificent courage and persistence brought her to the top, not only of Paris, but of the world, and made her one of the most known and notable figures of her day. When she died, at eighty, she was still a superbly creative spirit, capable of weaving life out of her vitals with a gorgeous sheen of silken splendor.

My concern is not so much with Sarah Bernhardt's art in the abstract as with her human personality and characteristics, but it should be recognized and established at the beginning that, however different critics may estimate her various impersonations, she was a most important factor in the dramatic life of her day. She had an immense influence on the art of acting, on the methods of play-writing, on the forms of stage production, and the history of the theater for the last fifty years could hardly be written without her. Above all, it is necessary, in connection with her art, to take into account the peculiar elements of her material personality, her extreme slenderness, giving an ethereal quality to everything she did, her mobility, her sensibility, her subtlety and power of adaptation. To some of us it appeared that there was just the suggestion of something hard and cynical about her, even of something common, but many of her admirers do not seem to have felt this, and in any event the drawbacks were lost in the charm, a charm summed up and epitomized in the voice, the voice of gold, which has been eulogized by so many critics and sung by so many poets. We do not generally consider Mr. Lytton Strachey inclined to excessive enthusiasm, but even he breaks out into lyrical raptures over the voice of Sarah Bernhardt, whether in its sweetness or still more in its power: 'The secret of that astounding utterance baffles the imagination. The words boomed and crashed with a superhuman resonance which shook the spirit of the hearer like a leaf in the wind. The *voix d'or* has often been raved over; but in Sarah Bernhardt's voice there was more than gold, there was thunder and lightning, there was heaven and hell.' [1]

When we turn from the abstract artist to the human being, we are on more tangible ground. In the first place Sarah was a worker, a tremendous, natural worker, who set out to do things, and did them, and got them done. The instinct of work may have been somewhat whimsical and erratic, especially in the earlier days. When George Sand is trying to get a play produced at the Odéon, during Sarah's apprenticeship, she complains that the actress 'does not work and thinks only of amusing herself.' [2] Again, there was a furious rush, a sense of constant hurry and pressure, about the woman's life at all times, which sometimes suggests that there may have been more bustle than actual labor. What a vivid picture does Claretie give of that driven, crowded, breathless existence: 'When she returned from the theater, doing a bit of sculpture, a bit of painting, receiving her friends, posing for a painter or a photographer, giving literary advice to the unpublished poets who brought her manuscripts.' [3] Or again, there is the single illuminating incident of the English teacher, who was engaged in haste because Sarah wanted to act Shakespeare in his own language. 'But I can give you only a half-hour a day,' said the actress. 'Will that be enough?' And when told it would be, she casually explained that it would have to be at half-past two in the morning, as every other minute was filled. [4]

Yet, for all this apparent superficial confusion, good observers insist upon the enormous power of accomplishment. Take memory. Sarah could learn any part in a few rehearsals, and she never forgot it, when she wanted it. So with everything. When tremendous, concentrated, intelligent, even systematic effort was called for, it was always forthcoming, and the results were both surprising and permanent. As Mr. Maurice Baring puts it: 'Her energy, the amount of hard work she accomplished were frightening to think of. Her recreation was change of work. She could command sleep when she wished, but she never rested. Yet she was fundamentally sensible.' [5] The last comment is one never to be lost sight of with Bernhardt.

One asks oneself how much abstract, theoretical thinking she did about her art. In the rush and tumult of her life general ideas somehow seem to find little place. At least I get little suggestion of them. It does not appear that she ever had much formal education, or that she ever read at all widely or thought on general subjects of any kind, as for example Charlotte Cushman did. I am not sure that she even speculated much on the general principles of acting. Her little book on 'The Art of the Theatre' is extraordinarily acute in detail, but does not show the larger movement of psychological analysis. On the other hand, everything that keen perception, instinctive and subtle sympathy and comprehension, imaginative penetration, could do, was done immediately and with complete and finished effect.

For her art was essentially an art of instinct and sympathy. 'This woman acts with her heart and her whole vitality,' says Sarcey.[6] Her theory would not have been exactly that of Joseph Jefferson, who said, 'For myself I know that I act the best when

the heart is warm and the head is cool.' ⁷ Sarah
could keep her head cool enough when she chose.
But she wanted to be aroused, stirred, excited, fired,
inspired, by the situation and the circumstances,
and then she could throw herself into the character
with all the power and the energy that were in her.
As she puts it, in 'The Art of the Theatre': 'Whatever I have to impart in the way of anguish, of
passion, or of joy, comes to me during rehearsal in
the very action of the play. There is no need to cast
about for an attitude, or a cry, or anything else.
You must be able to find everything you want on
the stage in the excitement created by the general
collaboration. Actors who stand in front of a mirror to strike an attitude or try to fall down on the
carpet of the room are fools.' ⁸

Sarah Bernhardt had in a high degree the artist's
peculiar combination of sensibility to the beautiful
with the eager desire to create it. The ordinary
person, even when richly endowed with such sensibility, is content to let beauty come to him, to open
his senses to it, to absorb it and appreciate it and
forget it. But such perception at once and at all
times stimulates the artist to assert his own power
and personality in the production of beauty of his
own. So it was with Bernhardt. This desire even

took varied artistic forms. Sometimes she was determined to paint, busied herself with lines and colors till it seemed as if the theater was forgotten. Again, it was all sculpture, and curiously enough, another great tragic actress, Sarah Siddons, also in her old age developed a passion for working with clay. In the later Sarah the passion was very real and very lasting, witness her own account of her absorption: 'I kept no clock, not even a watch with me. I wanted to ignore the time of day altogether. ... How often I neither breakfasted nor dined, having simply forgotten all about it.' [9] It is characteristic of her that when she began a work of this kind, she finished it. She may have destroyed it afterwards, as the bust of Rothschild, which she smashed before his face, just when he had drawn her a check for ten thousand francs. But, good, bad, or indifferent, the work had to be done.

After all, however, these things were avocations and side issues. And her real life, her real existence, was on the stage. It is probably true of all artists that in a sense they do not live for themselves at all, that is, they do not give themselves up to pure, simple, intense, natural living for itself. There is always the sense of the 'double life,' which Sarah suggests in the subtitle of her Memoirs, always the consciousness of standing apart and observing one-self, of getting out of every passion and experience something to enlarge and enrich and develop the permanent artistic production that is all you care for. As Goethe put it, 'whenever I had a sorrow, I made a poem.' The result of this is a curious blend of reality and artificiality, varying in its proportions with the type of artist and with the individual, but probably most intense and most complicated of all with the actor, whose everyday life is so fleeting and uncertain and whose artistic life is so dominating and so pervasive. This quick and constant and complicated interchange of life and art is admirably suggested in Mrs. Siddons's confidence, as recorded in the Diary of Moore. 'Among other reasons for her regret at leaving the stage was that she always found in it a vent for her private sorrows which enabled her to bear them better; and often she got credit for the truth and feeling of her acting when she was doing nothing more than relieving her own heart of its grief.' [10] But certainly no artist, theatri-cal or other, ever effected a more complete inter-mingling and reaction of art and life than did Sarah Bernhardt. When she was off the stage, she always seemed to be acting; she always seemed to be liv-ing when she was on it.

II

Which does not mean that she did not live at all times with passionate veracity, and most of all the veracity was evident in the variety of her human relations. The temperament of the artist appears again I think especially in these, because I do not find that she really lived very much for any one but herself, or ever much lost her identity in that of any one else. But human beings were immensely necessary to her, in all possible connections, and if she did not give to them, she took from them, enormously, which, after all, involves a certain amount of giving.

Her family relations were curious. Her father was little more than a phantom. But her mother and her two sisters she was very close to at times, close to, yet worlds remote from. For they were all much like butterflies — when they were not like cats: they flitted, and quivered, and kissed, with sudden, astonishing propensities to scratch, as in Sarah herself. Nothing can be more significant than the little touch of Sarah's mother forgiving her sister on her deathbed. 'You do forgive me? The priest has bidden you to forgive me. You do forgive me?' 'Yes — camel!' " Such was Madame Bernhardt, and it can hardly be wondered that Sarah never got much satisfaction out of her.

Did she get much more out of her son, Maurice? Madame Berton, who has narrated Sarah's career with such minute, if not always very amicable, fidelity, insists that mother love was an overpowering and developing motive, and that the necessity of providing for her child was the mainspring of Sarah's devotion to her art. This is absurd, and all the children in the world would not have made her an actress, or prevented her being one. No doubt she was attached to Maurice. No doubt she was proud of him. No doubt she made sacrifices for him, after her fashion. The risk of her life to get him out of her burning apartment, as she did, in spite of her inborn horror of fire, was just the sort of thing that would have appealed to her at any time. But I do not gather that Maurice's companionship or sympathy really meant much in her existence. Perhaps she got as much out of him as parents usually do.

In the same way with Sarah's innumerable love-affairs, it does not appear that she ever really gave herself, or lost herself. There was infinite curiosity, eagerness, the sense of adventure, the desire to probe, to investigate, to explore, other thoughts, other hearts, other souls; there is no suggestion of complete abandon or self-forgetfulness. Perhaps to the very end Sarah retained something of the cynical childish impression that she imbibed from her mother's very promiscuous establishment: 'My mother's house was always full of men, and the more I saw of them, the less I liked them.' [12]

Even the eccentric marriage to the Greek actor Damala in 1882 does not seem to be any marked exception to the rule. It was simply a *toquade*, a wild, erratic fancy. Sarah took a notion to run off with the man to England, broke all her engagements, and paid a huge forfeit on her contract. [13] She sent two telegrams to Sardou. The first ran: 'I am going to die and my greatest regret is not having created your play. Adieu!' The second followed: 'I am not dead, I am married.' [14] And when Sardou asked her later why the devil she married, she replied: 'Why? Because it was the only thing I never had done.' [15] She stuck to her drug-besotted husband till his death seven years later, with obstinate racial loyalty that was very impressive. But the whole affair seems to have been mainly a conflict of sex-vanities, in which Sarah got rather the worst of it.

The two things that are really significant about

Sarah's amorous connections are first that she loved for love or for character or for position, but not for money: her lovers were not idle sons of wealthy men. And secondly, her love appears to have inspired, ennobled, enriched life, instead of degrading it. As Madame Berton puts it, admirably: 'The influence she exerted on her century in matters of art was incalculable. To painters she would say: "If you love me, then paint a masterpiece and dedicate it to me." To poets she would say: "If it is true that you love me, you will write a poem about me that will live when we both are dead."' [16] And Alexandre Dumas fils once summed up the same thing: 'She drives me mad when I am with her. She is all temperament and no heart; but when she is gone, how I work! How I *can* work!' [17] While the larger quality of Sarah's influence is well indicated in Maurice Baring's enthusiastic statement of the trace she left in all the art aspects of her time: 'Eliminate these things and you eliminate one of the sources of inspiration of modern art; you take away something from D'Annunzio's poetry, from Maeterlinck's prose, from Moreau's pictures; you destroy one of the mainsprings of Rostand's work; you annihilate some of the colors of modern painting and you stifle some of the notes of modern music; for in all these you can trace in varying degrees the subtle, unconscious influence of Sarah Bernhardt.' [18]

So, in all the human relations, more intimate or more remote, it is the same story, always the artist, stimulating, inspiring, but infinitely curious, gathering, not giving, needing, and using, and absorbing, and throwing aside, not so much from deliberate selfishness or cruelty, as from immense, unbroken preoccupation with the one, huge, engrossing object of life. Sarah had, it appears, at all times the power of attaching, devoting human beings to her service with an unreasoning, animal devotion. 'Even the stage hands adored her,' says Claretie. [19] When an old maid left her, worn out with service, she assured her mistress, 'If madam is ever in difficulties, we shall remember that we owe her everything: she shall have our best chamber at her disposal.' [20] And the faithful attendant, Madame Guérard, who appears to have been bullied and browbeaten without much mercy, yet stuck to her friend with a fidelity, an assiduity, and a discerning tenderness that nothing could shake or break.

Through it all, for good, bad, or indifferent, you feel that with Sarah the human element was the one thing that counted. If it was lovers, she must have the best, and as many as possible. If it was admirers and spectators, let them throng to her in untold thousands. If the War came, in 1870, or in 1914, still there were human beings to be thought of and dealt with and appealed to, and in 1870 she gave up her art and threw herself into hospital work with the same furious ardor that she brought to the stage.

The human zest is so constant and so keen and so besetting that you wonder whether it left her time for anything else, whether the woman had any inner, solitary life at all. When she was alone, if she ever was, apparently she slept. To be sure, in one irritated moment, she cries out, in her Memoirs, 'I detest frequented walks, I adore deserted regions and solitary places.' [21] But this is only to make an effective antithesis, and I gravely doubt whether she ever relished solitude in her life. So with the things that go with solitude, for example, God. She had queer attacks of religion in her childhood, both in the convent and out of it. For a time she vibrated between the cloister and the stage. The stage instinct was probably at the bottom of both inclinations, and she herself frankly admits that there was little real devotion about her conventual fancies. She continued a devout Catholic, after her fashion, all her life, and died as one. But what the Almighty thought of her as an adherent, it may be easy to conjecture. And on the spiritual side her career hardly merits extensive study.

No, she was human, always intensely, passionately, collectively, extensively human, and all her wildest freaks and vagaries, her extraordinary whims and fancies and eccentricities, have some bearing on her human interest and are best understood in their human connection.

In a sense all these extravagances were genuine and spontaneous: they were native in the complicated tangle of Sarah Bernhardt's inheritance; but, whether trivial and insignificant or profound and far-reaching, they were always calculated to impress and startle and bewilder the human beings about her. If she went on a sleigh-ride in Canada, she would suddenly call to the driver to stop, rise in her place, throw off the robes, and fling herself out into a snowdrift, to stamp the image of her face and figure, like a child.[22] Of the same order was her balloon ascent, which astonished Paris and shocked the staid director of the Théâtre Français. So again the whole world was told of the coffin, which she had made and carried about with her

everywhere, sometimes sleeping in it or even cele-
brating an elaborate funeral service. And, like
Circe, she always had her strange herd of animals,
lizards, leopards, alligators, monkeys, lions, not to
speak of dogs and cats, which she cherished and
petted, partly from genuine love of the creature
life and partly to torment and perplex everybody
who had to come into contact with her.

All these actual facts of extravagance were amplified into a mad halo of fiction and legend, like
the story that Sarah set her own apartment on fire,
to get the insurance and make publicity, and endless others. And where she did not invent or encourage these tales, she at any rate reveled in them,
as is clearly indicated in the confession of her
Memoirs: 'Although I had then fully reached the
age of reason, I took pleasure in this mischievous
childishness, which I always regret afterwards, and
always renew, since even to-day, after the days,
the weeks, the months, the years that I have lived,
I take infinite pleasure in playing tricks.' [23] The
notable point is that through all this mad, freakish
frolic the one thing that is always taken seriously
is Sarah herself. There is not a trace of the subtle
dissolution of self, of the vast sense of personal insignificance, which haunted, for example, Charles

Lamb, or Sarah's contemporary on the stage, Joseph Jefferson. Self is the one thing that is not laughable under any circumstances. The universe is Bernhardt, and Bernhardt is the universe: there is absolutely nothing else.

III

What is most interesting and significant about all these freaks and extravagances of Sarah's is their value for publicity and advertising. As it happened, her career ran side by side with that of Barnum, the great wizard of notoriety creation, and with the enormous development of newspaper activity that characterized the middle of the nineteenth century. Certainly no actor ever before had had a tithe of the general printed notice that fell to Sarah Bernhardt, and it was said that if the newspaper comments she received were placed end to end, they would have reached around the world. [24] The peculiar characteristics of her personality were registered and trumpeted and enlarged, till it seemed as if Barnum could have done no more for his most cherished monstrosity.

Yet all the time it must be remembered that Sarah was not only a popular phenomenon, but an artist of real genius, a great actress, a creator, and a poet. That is what gives her case its importance and curiosity. Every possible use was made of ingenious advertising, but the thing advertised was worth while and of enduring value. Of course Whistler offers a somewhat similar instance. The genius was undoubted, but the methods of getting it before the public were sometimes startling, to say the least. Perhaps one may adduce Mr. Bernard Shaw in the same line. Mr. Shaw's genius is as real as Bernhardt's or Whistler's, but neither of them was a more skillful artist in drawing public attention. And one wonders sometimes what would have been Shakespeare's attitude towards such procedure. Shakespeare was a shrewd man of business and the hard experience of life had taught him the value of coin and the difficulty of getting it. Would he have utilized publicity to the full and developed unheard-of resources in it? If he had, we may at least be sure that he would have done it with a smile at himself, like Whistler and Mr. Shaw, and unlike Bernhardt.

There are various interesting questions in regard to Bernhardt's attitude in this connection. First, how far were the eccentricities cultivated and developed with a consciousness of their publicity value? I have already insisted that they were

native and inborn. So they undoubtedly were. At
the same time, human nature, Sarah's human
nature above all, being what it is, when the profit of
such things became increasingly obvious, it was
hardly to be supposed that the tendency to them
would diminish: it certainly did not. Just the working of the tendency is delicately suggested in the
remark of Arsène Houssaye: 'She has her enemies
and her critics, but the more of her statues you
break, the more there are made for her. Moreover,
she takes a hand in the matter herself.' [25]

Again, one asks not only how far did Sarah deliberately supply the material for the notoriety, but
how far did she encourage and support it? She
knew perfectly well that the newspapers and the
world rang with her oddities and vagaries. Just
how far did her hand in the matter reach? It is
difficult to say exactly. In her Memoirs she of
course denies any interference whatever. What had
she to do with it? 'When you think that my first
title to publicity was my extraordinary slenderness
and my fragile health!... Was it simply to be no-
torious that I was so slight and so thin and so
weak?' [26] The same plea is frequently urged in
varying forms. Yet it is hard to believe that the
publicity would have flourished without the artist's

connivance and one inclines to think that, like Shaw and Whistler, she was quite as much of an artist in getting her work known as in creating it.

Again, there is the question, how far she not only stimulated publicity but enjoyed it. No doubt there were times when the boredom was intolerable. Reporters, especially in America, were silly and intrusive and wearisome. Absurd stories, like that of her adventure with the whale, were repeated and exaggerated to the point of nausea. Publicity carried with it its necessary burden not only of tediousness but of actual hostility and spite: 'Ah! success! With what a strong chain it rivets one and how painful it sometimes is. How many times the noise made around me, the good said in my favor, the bad written against me have invaded my tranquillity and created an atmosphere of battle. Jealous friends, secret or open enemies, into what turmoil have you not often thrust me! And how many times have I not been accused of an immoderate liking for advertisement.' [27] But it has not yet been discovered that these drawbacks of glory were sufficient to induce any one to throw it away.

The final question is, how much Sarah profited practically by the huge notoriety, and the answer is that her financial gains were constant and very considerable. She was clear-headed and cold-blooded, when it suited her, and she knew just when, just where, and just how the francs and the dollars came. Madame Berton asserts that 'altogether she brought back considerably more than six million dollars' from the United States, [28] and if this is somewhat fantastic, the actual product must have been large enough. The figures given by one of her managers, Schurman, are most impressive, and equally so is one little financial scene narrated in her Memoirs: 'In the saloon of my car Abbey and Jarrett show me the balance-sheet for the sixty-two representations, given since we left home, amounting to 225,459 dollars; that is to say, one million, one hundred and thirty-seven thousand francs, or an average of eighteen thousand, three hundred, and forty-three francs for each performance.' [29]

And every bit of the money was needed and spent, for, earn as vastly as she could, her outlay was usually in excess of her earning. To be sure, her personal tastes were not in all ways extravagant. She was temperate in eating and drinking, all her life was a strict vegetarian and attributed her enduring vigor largely to this regimen. But she could not hold on to money, did not care to. She lavished it on whims of all sorts, took a pride and pleasure in doing so. She lent and gave as freely as she spent for herself, so that finally, in a crisis she murmured, 'All my life, it seems, I have been making money for others to spend.' [30] Always she was piling up obligations and then discharging them and then piling up more. How vivid is the picture that Claretie gives of these financial comings and goings. 'She laughed at everything, with the utmost cheerfulness. In her dressing-room the money that she daily received evaporated like the solution of gold under *aqua regia*. During the entr'acte there was, as it were, a hand-to-mouth distribution of her daily receipts in all sorts of fractions, by hundred francs, by twenty francs. Fifteen hundred francs was paid her. Quick! the distribution, the pillage, the slaughter! Poor woman! "Here, you, take this! Carry it to the coiffeur." "Ah! Something on account for X. — something for Z. — Well, what is it now? T. wrote this morning. I'll send him this, and he will be patient a little longer." Then, laughing still, "What have I got left? Fifteen francs. Bah! With fifteen francs you don't die of hunger. But just go and change this five franc piece for me. I've got to have some change to pay the cabman." So it went every night.' [31]

It was not exactly that she did not have the making of a business woman in her. It is curious to think how much of that woman there was in these great tragic actresses. Mrs. Siddons was a hard money-maker, who had the keenest eye for a bargain. You have only to read Charlotte Cushman's manuscript letters in the Shaw Collection to see what her business habits were. And Sarah was as keen as either of them to know a good trade and follow it up. But her Bohemian training made her incurably erratic, and still more, she took a pride in her financial indifference. The training and the pride both show in her careless account of her own carelessness: 'I promise everything with the firm intention of executing my promise and two hours after I have forgotten everything. If some friend recalls it to me, I tear my hair and make up excuses to patch up my neglect. I complicate my life with all sorts of useless frets. So it has been since — always, and so it will be to the end.' [32]

And this woman undertook to manage theaters, just as a somewhat similar dreamer, Edwin Booth, did, but curiously enough, she was far more successful than Booth. The erratic habits always seemed destined to wreck her. As Claretie puts it, of an early venture: 'Directress of La Porte Saint-

Martin, this magnificent lunatic, who never knew how to direct her own life! In eight days she accepted eighteen plays, all sublime, and all to be played by Sarah Bernhardt, each three hundred times running. All this to end in a situation which reeked with bankruptcy and the odor of disaster.' [33] What saved her, what enabled her to do what she wanted in the world was her power over people. She got the actors she wanted, she got the managers she wanted, she got the authors she wanted, and she made them all do what she wanted. That was perhaps her greatest gift and the richest instrument of her financial as of other success. I don't know anything in this line that has impressed me more than her conquest of Roosevelt. Naturally there was no sex in the matter, at least not directly, it was simply a case of one soul of power recognizing another. But she had a letter from Roosevelt which she treasured, and with reason: 'I have altered my plans so as to arrive in Paris after you return from Spain. I could not come to Paris and miss seeing my oldest and best friend there.' [34] And when she showed the letter to her friends, she murmured, perhaps with a certain reason also: 'Ah! but that man and I, we could rule the world!' [35]

With this magic gift of dominating and swaying

hearts, it was natural that fortunes should come to her as lightly as they departed. It seemed as if she had but to hold out her hand and money would flow into it. Only, as often as not, the hand was held out the wrong side up.

IV

But let no eager aspirant for dramatic success imagine that Sarah's career was an unbroken triumph or a shadowless course of easy felicity. It was far, far the contrary, and no doubt she often pictured it to herself as a series of struggles and difficulties and obstacles that had to be eluded or surmounted or blown or blasted away. As Maurice Baring describes it: 'The whole of Sarah Bernhardt's artistic life was a fight against apparently insurmountable difficulties.' [36]

There was health, and in the early years this seemed to be an insuperable obstacle to success. Sarah's voice was weak, and her extreme physical tenuity appeared to be incompatible with stage impressiveness. She was always fainting, or collapsing, or giving out in some way at inopportune moments. But she showed a superhuman skill in turning her very defects to excellences, and her own account of the triumph of spiritual resource over fleshly weakness is most extraordinary, above all, in just the touch of melodrama which is peculiarly characteristic. It seems that, in desperation over her failures and the disgust of Perrin, the director of the Français, she had made up her mind that she never could succeed, and one day, when she was playing the tragic rôle of Zaïre, she decided to throw herself into it with such fury of passion as in her exhausted state would necessarily be fatal. She carried out her suicidal determination to the full, pouring into the part a tempest of excitement which she thought she could not possibly survive. What happened? Not only did she achieve a sudden and immense success, but she found herself physically — or spiritually — remade. 'I hopped up lightly for the recall, and greeted the public without exhaustion, without weakness, quite ready to begin the play all over again. And I marked this performance with a white stone, for from that day on I understood that my vital forces were at the service of my brain. I had tried to follow the impulse of my intelligence, all the time believing that this impulse would be too violent for my physical energy to sustain it. And when I had done everything I tried to do, I found that the balance of mental and physical was perfect. Then I began to see the possibility of realizing what I had dreamed.'[37]

Again, there was the obstacle of stage fright, which haunted Sarah from the beginning to the end of her career. This took one of the most hampering and annoying forms for an actress, it affected her voice. As Sarcey expressed it, 'her teeth set sharply by a sort of unconscious contraction, and the words left her lips cut short and tense, with a harsh sonority. She recovered her natural voice only when she had succeeded in mastering her emotion.' [38] Sarah's own account of her experiences is much the same, though she distinguishes curiously between her early fear of simply not making herself heard at all in public and the later nervousness that overcame her when she began to be conscious of all the possibilities of failure. Once more curiously characteristic, however, is the fighting spirit in which she met this difficulty as well as others. Mrs. Siddons speaks of the peculiar resolution which came to her in exceptional crises, 'one of what I call my desperate tranquillities, which usually impress me under terrific circumstances.' [39] So with the other Sarah; when she had a struggle to face, she faced it, and never gave way: 'I who am so liable to stage fright had no fear, for with me stage fright assumes a curious form; in front of a public which I feel to be hostile for one reason or another, I am free from all stage fright; I have only one idea, one resolve: to subjugate the refractory audience. In front of a benevolent public, on the other hand, I am alarmed lest I should not come up to expectations and stage fright grips me imperiously.' [40] But the strain of the battle was exhausting, all the same: it was hard to say which took more out of you, the public that was benevolent or the public that was not, and the path to glory, whether it led to the grave or elsewhere, was one of incessant struggle and war.

There was war with the human elements about you, also, at all times, and of all human elements undoubtedly the most vexing and distracting was yourself, at any rate for one constituted as was Sarah Bernhardt. There was the petulant, devouring fury of her inborn temper, which she inherited from her mother. In her childhood her fits of frenzy developed into absolute collapse, and listen to her own account of one outburst of provocation with her sister in later years: 'When once we were in the carriage, I struck my little sister with such rage that Madame Guérard, terrified, covered her with her body and herself received my blows with my fists, my feet, with everything, for I rushed at her all over, mad with rage, with fury, and with shame.' [41] She not only had the fury of temper, she had a native quickness of tongue and a burning outspokenness, which fostered hostility even where she had no intention of doing so. As to whether she was fundamentally jealous of her fellows, there may be more question. She herself would never admit it, not having the charming candor which made Joseph Jefferson confess, 'In this case my rival was a good actor, but not too good to be jealous of me, and if our positions had been reversed, the chances are that I would have been jealous of him.' [42] Her bitter enemy, Marie Colombier, insists that 'she proved herself jealous of all her comrades, jealous even of her sisters.' [43] Probably she was not less inclined than others to dislike the success of her rivals and even to belittle it, for in this as in everything, she was constantly and enormously human.

In any case, with her temperament as it was, she had her difficulties with humanity, plenty of them, at all times and in all varieties. Perhaps the most of these were with her fellow actors. It must be admitted that in some cases she cherished long and loyal friendships. Her relation with Croizette, for years perhaps her most prominent competitor, seems to have been in the main friendly and even affectionate. And Sarah herself makes a very curious comment, that she finds much more pettiness and hostility and mean jealousy and spite from the men actors than from the women, who she says are in the main inclined to be friendly to her and to get along well. This was not always true, however, for it was an actual slap in the face, given to an older fellow actress, which drove Sarah from the Français in the early days, and long, long afterwards the same tendency to physical violence would break out when her nerves got too strained and the provocation too desperate. Also, there was the unseemly war of words and pamphlets between her and Marie Colombier, in which probably everybody was wrong and certainly everybody was unfortunate and indiscreet.

The relations with managers were no less complicated and difficult than with actors. But to keep well with managers was essential to one's bread and butter, and Sarah had always a shrewd sense of the importance of bread and butter as the first essential of life. Therefore her managerial history, though checkered by all sorts of flaws and breaks and disasters, was eminently practical. All the same, to have to rehearse her must have been an ordeal for any manager. She had her inspirations of genius, but to meet and deal with her whims and fancies was a task that at times assumed the proportions of nightmare.

If it was bad for the managers, it was much worse for the authors, since the manager has at least the power of his contract and his forfeit behind him. The poor author could hardly even suggest, he could only obey. How vividly does Claretie sum up the tragedy that rehearsal meant, after narrating various harrowing incidents in one particular case: 'These rehearsals, calculated to drive an author mad, achieved a real celebrity. With interpreters like this woman, who is nevertheless a great artist and in no sort of way a spiteful creature, the author's business becomes a torment. I had rather break stone on the roads than put Sarah Bernhardt through a rehearsal.' [44]

Yet was there ever an actress who made the reputation and fortune of more dramatic authors than Sarah Bernhardt did? Coppée and she first soared into glory together. Richepin and Lemaître owed their chief success to her. Dumas thought nothing of 'Camille' till she remade it and made it the triumph of two continents, and it was through her that 'Frou-Frou' became Meilhac and Halévy's masterpiece. Sardou gladly recognized that it was the adaptation of her genius to his that gave him wealth and credit and Rostand was almost her child as well as her lover.

With the critics the story is something the same. Newspaper criticism is the plague, the bane, the horror of every artist, but of the actor most of all, for with the actor it is always most cursory and generally least intelligent. Great actors are apt to proclaim their indifference to it, and also to devour every word of it with tortured curiosity. On the whole, Sarah Bernhardt was more fortunate than some others. Heaven knows, she got abuse and vilification enough, of her art, of her characters, of her extravagances and oddities. But the greatest critics of Paris were usually kind to her. Some were her lovers, some were her personal friends without being lovers, and the long, devoted, unloverlike attachment of the greatest genius among them, Jules Lemaître, is the best testimony to the finer qualities of Sarah's heart. All the same, criticism is a misery at the best. The artist could not flourish without it, but sometimes he feels that he can hardly exist with it, and what appears most fretting is the utter unintelligence of it. You could forgive these people anything, if only they would make the least effort to understand what you are trying to do.

So the life of the artist, especially of the dramatic artist, is a long struggle, and that of Sarah Bernhardt was no exception, rather a most vivid illustration, of the rule. There are times when the struggle seems intolerable, when the wisest falter and the bravest are ready to give up. Even the self-centered and self-assured Charlotte Cushman was overcome at moments and cries: 'Often, as I left the theater and compared my own acting with Rachel's, despair took possession of me and a mad impulse to end life and effort together.' [45] If we can accept her own accounts and those of others, Sarah was repeatedly at the point of suicide, and there is no more effective description of such a crisis than that given by George Sand, all the more important because it deals with Sarah's early, formative years and has a larger bearing on her character as well as on the special point involved: 'One evening "L'Autre" was being given at the Odéon. I looked in at Duquesnel's office and I found the whole theater in commotion. I was told that Sarah Bernhardt, who played Hélène with exquisite grace, had tried to poison herself. I went up to see her. I reasoned with her. I spoke of her son to whom she owed all her care and tenderness. I said everything that a woman and a mother could say in such a case. Sarah burst into tears. She assured me that she had a horror of the existence she had been leading hitherto, that nobody had ever spoken to her as I had done, and that my advice would never pass from her memory. A few days after this I got to the theater a little late. I met Sarah Bernhardt and her sister Jeanne on the staircase, both dressed like men and starting for the Bal Bullier. And this is all my remonstrances and my sermon came to. Let me repeat, look out for the women of the theater: they are at once more fascinating, more perverse, and more dangerous than any others.' [46]

The fascination and the perversity and the danger were certainly unlimited, and also the misery running to any point of despair and even suicide. What carried Sarah Bernhardt through it all to a triumphant consummation was the magnificent, vital energy and persistence of her character. You could not really discourage her, or dishearten her, or beat her, or kill her. From the beginning she was determined to succeed. 'Madame Sand,' she said, in the early days, 'I would rather die than not be the greatest actress in the world.' [47] Not only a great actress, you see, but the greatest actress in the world. And on the whole, for her day, she certainly was, and it was sheer will that did it, or at any rate will was the driving force, the same superb will that attracted her in Theodore Roosevelt and made her see herself and him as ruling the world.

It is impossible to give a more vigorous and telling picture of what this driving force was than her own, in association with the careless motto, *Quand même*: 'They knew that my device, *Quand même*, was not a matter of accident, but the result of deliberate reflection. My mother explained that at nine years old I adopted this device, after a mad leap over a ditch that no one could cross and to which my young cousin had challenged me. I had scratched my face, broken my wrist, bruised my whole body. And while they were carrying me home, I shouted, beside myself: "I will do it again, I will do it again, if he dares me again, and I will do all my life just what I will to do." ' [48] So she did, as far as a human being may. What gave more than mere erratic violence, more than mere chaotic tumult, to such furious exertion of the will for itself, was a certain pervading, if obscure, sense of the ideal behind it: 'My ideal?' said Sarah. 'My ideal? But I am still pursuing it. I shall pursue it until my last hour, and I feel that in the supreme moment I shall know the certainty of attaining it beyond the tomb.' [49]

V

The result of this determined ambition and prolonged ideal effort was a career of triumph and success hardly paralleled by any other artist either on the stage or off it. And the peculiar quality of Sarah Bernhardt's success was its inexhaustible novelty, its endless series of developments and surprises and renewals. She did not attain one great climax and stay there or gradually fade away from it. She did not identify herself with one great part and remain identified with it till she died, like Joseph Jefferson. She was vital, spontaneous, creative, to an extraordinary extent, was always attempting new things and achieving them. As Mr. Baring expresses it admirably: 'She spent her life in making discoveries and in surprising the public and her critics by finding out what she could not do and in immediately doing it.' [50]

This element of surprise, of perpetually revealing herself, even to herself, is notable all through her life, in the later years just as much as in the earlier. At the Odéon the managers thought nothing of her. She discovered Coppée, and triumphed. She went to the Français, and repeated the story. She went to London and became the star of the company. She left the Français in 1880. Everybody thought it was her ruin. Instead, she went to America and became the star of the world. When she came back to Paris, the critics thought her head would be turned and she would be no longer capable of serious art. Yet when she played 'Phèdre,' in 1893, at nearly fifty, Sarcey and Lemaître raved over her and declared that she was younger and more beautiful than she had ever been. Then she began all over again with the creations of Sardou, a new drama and a new style of acting. When this wore thin in Paris, she carried it to America and to Australia, and came back to France to develop a new author and a new art with the romantic plays of Rostand. She lost a leg, and an ordinary actress would have dropped into the infirmary and the invalid chair. Not Sarah. She acted with her voice and her soul, not with her legs, and she went right on. When she produced Racine's 'Athalie,' in 1920, after the War, every theater in Paris was closed, so that her fellow actors might see her perform once more. On the very eve of her death, when she was nearly eighty, she acted for the movies. The doctors said it would kill her. Perhaps it did.

What did she care? She was bound to die fighting.

The priceless privilege of this element of perpetual renewal in Sarah's life was that she escaped the decay and self-survival that disfigure the old age of so many artists, actors, and others. Hear what Mrs. Kemble writes of her aunt, Mrs. Siddons: 'What a price my Aunt Siddons has paid for her great celebrity! Weariness, vacuity, and utter deadness of spirit. The cup has been so highly flavored that life is absolutely without sorrow or sweetness to her now, nothing but tasteless insipidity. She has stood on a pinnacle till all things have come to look flat and dreary, mere shapeless, colorless, level monotony to her. Poor woman! What a fate to be condemned to! and yet how she has been envied as well as admired!' [51] There was nothing of this decay about Sarah, nothing but superb, mature power and exuberant energy to the very end. Again, there is no trace in her of the haunting melancholy that clung to Edwin Booth even in his days of greatest triumph, or of the subtle sense of dreamy emptiness that Jefferson found in the greatest successes of the stage. Just because she took herself and all her effort so seriously there was no sense of hollowness or emptiness in it at all. You have to look long and closely for

even a suggestion of the satiety that almost always
follows great spiritual strain and unalloyed success,
as in her brief beautiful phrase, 'Tout passe, tout
casse, tout lasse, all fails, all stales, all pales,' or in
Claretie's story of her stopping in the midst of a
triumphant rehearsal to complain of the unsatis-
factoriness of her lot. To be sure, she had everything. 'But the end, the end! It is the end that
counts. It is the finish that ought to be dramatic
and enthralling. Take Rochefort — killed by a ball
at the moment of his escape. What an admirable
death! That was a climax. Drama! Mystery! Tell
me, how do you think I shall end?' [52]

Yet even here, in the touch of disgust, you get the
vitality, the mystery, the suggestion of the unknown that gave a thrill to it all. As she herself
puts it, most effectively, in her Memoirs: 'Always,
when circumstances arise to disturb the current of
my life, I at first have an impulse of shrinking. For
a second I cling to what actually is; then I fling
myself headlong into what may be.... All at once
what is becomes for me what was, and I cherish it
with a tender emotion, as if it were something dead.
But I adore what is to be. It is the unknown, the
alluring, the mysterious. I believe always that it
will be the unheard of, and I shudder from head to

foot, with a delicious surmise.' [53] Always adventure, discovery, experiment, always probe the unknown and reach out for its deepest secrets, *Quand même, Quand même*, no matter what happens, and make it your highest pride to go out of life with the same magnificent zest that you brought into it.

So, with this whole company of Daughters of Eve, you feel that they all had a touch of *Quand même*, they were all adventurers, all free, joyous, careless experimenters with life. The brilliant Ninon, yes, even the apparently sane and judicious Maintenon, the madly mystical Guyon, the intensely passionate, concentrated Lespinasse, the high-spirited, rollicking Catherine, the idealist Sand, the freakish, fantastic Bernhardt, every single one of them was animated by the thrill, the enthusiasm, the glory of the superb stanza of the Marquis of Montrose, who might have been a lover for any of them:

> He either fears his fate too much,
> Or his deserts are small,
> Who dares not put it to the touch,
> To gain or lose it all.

THE END

NOTES

NOTES

THE titles of books most frequently cited are prefixed to each chapter with abbreviations used.

I: NINON DE LENCLOS

Austin, Cecil, *The Immortal Ninon*.   Austin

Lenclos, Ninon de, *Correspondance Authentique*, edited by Émile Colombey.   *Correspondance*

Voltaire, *Œuvres Complètes*, 1880 edition.   Voltaire

1. Austin, p. 9.
2. In *Correspondance*, p. 222.
3. In *Correspondance*, p. 219.
4. In *Correspondance*, p. 62.
5. Voltaire, vol. XXIII, p. 510.
6. Austin, p. 56.
7. In *Correspondance*, p. 235.
8. In Sainte-Beuve, *Causeries du Lundi*, vol. IV, p. 140.
9. M. le Baron Walckenaer, *Mémoires Touchant la Vie et les Écrits de Marie de Rabutin-Chantal, Marquise de Sévigné*, vol. I, p. 241.
10. In Austin, pp. 178, 179.
11. *Correspondance*, p. 57.
12. Voltaire, vol. XXIII, p. 509.
13. In *Correspondance*, p. 208.
14. In *Correspondance*, p. 12.
15. *Correspondance*, p. 60.
16. Walckenaer, *Mémoires* (as above), vol. I, p. 241.
17. Austin, p. 130.
18. *Correspondance*, p. 110.
19. Châteauneuf, in *Correspondance*, p. 219.
20. To Marquise de Villette, August 16, 1705? *Correspondance*, p. 174.
21. In *Correspondance*, p. 204.
22. *Ibid.*

NOTES

23. In *Correspondance*, p. 210.
24. In *Correspondance*, p. 227.
25. In Sainte-Beuve, *Nouveaux Lundis*, vol. XIII, p. 442.
26. Saint-Évremond to Ninon, 1697, *Correspondance*, p. 118.
27. Saint-Évremond to Ninon, 1687, *Correspondance*, p. 113.
28. To Saint-Évremond, 1690, *Correspondance*, p. 132.
29. To Saint-Évremond, 1690, *Correspondance*, p. 133.
30. Sainte-Beuve, *Portraits Contemporains*, vol. V, p. 461.
31. *As You Like It*, II, VII.
32. Montaigne, *Essais*, book III, chapter II, edition Louandre, vol. III, p. 347.
33. In Austin, p. 258.
34. Matthew Arnold, Sonnet, *To a Friend*.
35. *Antigone*, line 523.

II: MADAME DE MAINTENON

Geffroy, A., *Madame de Maintenon d'Après Sa Correspondance Authentique.*   Geffroy

Maintenon, Madame de, *Correspondance Générale*, 4 vols.
Correspondance Générale

Maintenon, Madame de, *Lettres* (Choisies), 2 vols. (Collection pour les Jeunes Filles).   *Lettres*

Maintenon, Madame de, *Lettres Historiques et Édifiantes*, 2 vols.   *Lettres Historiques*

1. *Correspondance Générale*, vol. I, p. I.
2. To Gobelin, July 24, 1674, *Correspondance Générale*, vol. I, p. 208.
3. Conversation with Madame Glapion, 1707, *Lettres Historiques*, vol. II, p. 215.
4. To Madame de Brinon, August 24, 1693, *Lettres Historiques*, vol. I, p. 312.
5. Conversation with Madame Glapion, September, 1708, *Lettres*, vol. II, p. 88.
6. September 9, 1698, *Lettres*, vol. I, p. 221.
7. Conversation with Madame Glapion, November 9, 1702, *Lettres Historiques*, vol. II, p. 102.

NOTES

8. Conversation with Madame Glapion, April 4, 1705, *Lettres*, vol. II, p. 44.

9. To Madame de Ventadour, February, 1692, *Lettres*, vol. I, p. 154.

10. Gaston Boissier, *Saint-Simon*, p. 147.

11. Théophile Lavallée, *Madame de Maintenon et La Maison Royale de Saint-Cyr*, p. 83.

12. *Lettres Historiques*, vol. I, p. 127.

13. Conversation with Madame Glapion, 1708, *Lettres*, vol. II, p. 89.

14. To Gobelin, September 13, 1674, *Correspondance Générale*, vol. I, p. 221.

15. To Gobelin, March, 1675, *Lettres*, vol. I, p. 27.

16. To Madame de Jas, October 15, 1697, *Lettres Historiques*, vol. II, p. 25.

17. Madame de Sévigné to Madame de Grignan, February 26, 1672, *Lettres de Madame de Sévigné* (smaller edition), vol. II, p. 62.

18. To Madame de Berval, *Lettres Historiques*, vol. I, p. 243.

19. Conversation with Madame Glapion, 1707, *Lettres Historiques*, vol. II, p. 213.

20. In Lavallée, *La Maison de Saint-Cyr*, p. 28.

21. To Dames de St. Louis, in *Lettres Historiques*, vol. II, p. 74.

22. *Correspondance Générale*, vol. II, p. 345.

23. *Mémoires de Saint-Simon* (smaller edition), vol. V, p. 137.

24. To Bishop of Châlons, August 18, 1695, *Correspondance Générale*, vol. IV, p. 12.

25. To Duc de Noailles, January 23, 1712, Geffroy, p. 296.

26. To Princesse des Ursins, September 18, 1713, Geffroy, p. 332.

27. July 9, 1714, *Lettres*, vol. II, p. 148.

28. To Madame de Veilhant, May 29, 1692, *Lettres*, vol. I, p. 160.

29. To D'Aubigné, September 25, 1679, *Lettres*, vol. I, p. 66.

30. To Pontchartrain, 1690, *Correspondance Générale*, vol. III, p. 258.

31. *Instruction*, 1709, Geffroy, p. 23.

32. In *Mémoires et Lettres Inédites de Mademoiselle d'Aumale*, printed by Haussonville et Hanotaux, *Souvenirs de Madame de Maintenon*, p. 52.

33. *Madame de Maintenon à Saint-Cyr*, in above, p. 248.

34. To Madame de Brinon, April, 1683, *Correspondance Générale*, vol. ii, p. 292.

35. To her intendant, Manceau, 1694, *Lettres*, vol. i, p. 171.

36. Sainte-Beuve, *Causeries du Lundi*, vol. iv, p. 290.

37. *Mémoires de Mademoiselle d'Aumale* (as above), p. xxiv.

38. To Gobelin, July 24, 1674, *Correspondance Générale*, vol. i, p. 206.

39. Conversation with Madame Glapion, October, 1708, *Lettres Historiques*, vol. ii, p. 276.

40. To Dames de St. Louis, *Lettres Historiques*, vol. ii, p. 75.

41. To Gobelin, August 1, 1674, *Lettres*, vol. i, p. 18.

42. Conversation with Madame Glapion, October 18, 1716, *Lettres Historiques*, vol. ii, p. 456.

43. To Madame de Saint-Périer, October 21, 1708, in Madame de Maintenon, *Lettres sur l'Éducation des Filles*, p. 379.

44. Questions to Bishop of Chartres, *Lettres Historiques*, vol. i, p. 499.

III: MADAME GUYON

Guyon, Madame J. B. de La Mothe, *Lettres Chrétiennes et Spirituelles*, 1768, 5 vols.   *Lettres Spirituelles*

Guyon, Madame J. B. de La Mothe, *Les Opuscules Spirituelles*, 1790, 2 vols.   *Opuscules*

Guyon, Madame J. B. de La Mothe, *Vie, Écrite par elle-même*, 1791, 3 vols.   *Vie*

Lemaître, Jules, *Fénelon*.   Lemaître

Masson, Maurice, *Fénelon et Madame Guyon*.   Masson

1. *Vie*, vol. i, p. 29.

2. *Vie*, vol. i, p. 26.

3. *Vie*, vol. i, p. 45.

4. *Vie*, vol. i, p. 58.

5. *Vie*, vol. i, p. 43.

6. To Fénelon, Masson, p. 278.

7. *Instruction Chrétienne*, *Opuscules*, vol. ii, p. 436.

8. *Vie*, vol. iii, p. 261.

NOTES

9. *Vie*, vol. I, p. 199.
10. *Instruction Chrétienne, Opuscules*, vol. II, p. 435.
11. *Vie*, vol. I, p. 185.
12. *Vie*, vol. I, p. 21.
13. Madame Guyon, *Discours Chrétiens et Spirituels*, vol. I, p. 282.
14. Quoted by Madame Guyon, in *Justification de Sa Doctrine*, vol. II, p. 308.
15. *Lettres Spirituelles*, vol. III, p. 624.
16. *Lettres Spirituelles*, vol. I, p. 408.
17. *Les Torrents Spirituelles*, in *Opuscules*, vol. I, p. 218.
18. Voltaire to D'Argental, June 22, 1764, *Correspondance de Voltaire*, edition 1880, vol. XI, p. 249.
19. *De la Voie et de la Réunion de l'Âme à Dieu, Opuscules*, vol. II, p. 326.
20. *Les Torrents Spirituelles, Opuscules*, vol. I, p. 154.
21. *Lettres Spirituelles*, vol. V, p. 553.
22. Quoted in Lyman P. Powell, *Christian Science, The Faith and Its Founder*, p. 74.
23. *Lettres Spirituelles*, vol. III, p. 261.
24. *Lettres Spirituelles*, vol. III, p. 634.
25. *Lettres Spirituelles*, vol. V, p. 496.
26. *Lettres Spirituelles*, vol. I, p. 109.
27. In Lemaître, p. 215.
28. In Lemaître, p. 240.
29. To Fénelon, Masson, p. 16.
30. *Vie*, vol. II, p. 133.
31. Autobiographical Fragment, in Masson, p. 6.
32. *Vie*, vol. II, p. 28.
33. Autobiographical Fragment, in Masson, p. 12.
34. *The Imitation of Christ*, book III, chapter 31.
35. Pascal, *Pensées*, XXIV, 70.
36. Arthur Schopenhauer, *The World as Will and Idea* (translation Haldane and Kemp), vol. I, p. 532.
37. *Lettres Spirituelles*, vol. III, p. 119.
38. *Les Torrents Spirituelles, Opuscules*, vol. I, p. 255.

NOTES

IV: MADEMOISELLE DE LESPINASSE

Lespinasse, Mademoiselle de, *Lettres* (edition Asse, 1906).

Lettres

Lespinasse, Mademoiselle de, *Lettres Inédites* (edition Henry, 1887).

Lettres Inédites

Lespinasse, Mademoiselle de, *Nouvelles Lettres*, 1920.

Nouvelles Lettres

1. Sainte-Beuve, *Causeries du Lundi*, vol. ii, p. 111.
2. To Condorcet, October 19, 1773, *Lettres Inédites*, p. 109.
3. *Ibid.*
4. Madame du Deffand to le Chevalier d'Aydie, July 14, 1755, in *Correspondance de Madame du Deffand* (edition Lescure), vol. i, p. 230.
5. In *Lettres*, p. 347.
6. *Lettres de Madame du Deffand à Horace Walpole* (edition Toynbee), vol. iii, p. 218.
7. La Harpe, *Correspondance Littéraire*, vol. i, p. 386.
8. In *Lettres*, p. xxi.
9. In *Lettres*, p. xxii.
10. In *Lettres*, p. 358.
11. In *Lettres*, p. 346.
12. To Guibert, September 19, 1774, *Lettres*, p. 101.
13. In *Lettres*, p. 346.
14. *Ibid.*
15. La Harpe, *Correspondance Littéraire*, vol. i, p. 386.
16. To Guibert, 1774, *Lettres*, p. 57.
17. To Guibert, September 23, 1774, *Lettres*, p. 109.
18. To Condorcet, June 24, 1772, *Lettres Inédites*, p. 80.
19. To Guibert, 1774, *Lettres*, p. 77.
20. To Condorcet, May 4, 1771, *Lettres Inédites*, p. 60.
21. To Crillon, January 14, 1774, *Lettres Inédites*, p. 192.
22. Edmond et Jules de Goncourt, *La Femme au XVIII Siècle*, p. 427.
23. To Condorcet, May, 1775, *Lettres Inédites*, p. 149.
24. In *Nouvelles Lettres*, p. 278.
25. *Ibid.*, p. 290.

26. To Condorcet, April 5, 1773, *Lettres Inédites*, p. 103.
27. To Guibert, September 22, 1774, *Lettres*, p. 105.
28. Quoted in *Lettres Inédites*, p. 259.
29. To Condorcet, 1775, *Lettres Inédites*, p. 147.
30. To Guibert, May 23, 1773, *Lettres*, p. 4.
31. To Guibert, July 1, 1773, *Lettres*, p. 26.
32. To Guibert, July 1, 1773, *Lettres*, p. 27.
33. August 23, 1772, *Lettres Inédites*, p. 91.
34. To Condorcet, April 5, 1773, *Lettres Inédites*, p. 104.
35. To Guibert, August 8, 1773, *Lettres*, p. 39.
36. To Guibert, September 22, 1774, *Lettres*, p. 105.
37. To Guibert, 1775, *Lettres*, p. 192.
38. To Guibert, 1775, *Lettres*, p. 189.
39. To Crillon, January 14, 1774, *Lettres Inédites*, p. 192.
40. To Guibert, 1774, *Lettres*, p. 60.
41. To Guibert, 1775, *Lettres*, p. 191.
42. To Guibert, 1774, *Lettres*, p. 156.
43. To Guibert, 1774, *Lettres*, p. 87.
44. To Guibert, March, 1774, *Lettres*, p. 58.
45. To Condorcet, 1773, *Lettres Inédites*, p. 106.
46. To Guibert, 1776, *Lettres*, p. 308.
47. To Guibert, May 30, 1773, *Lettres*, p. 9.
48. To Guibert, August 15, 1773, *Lettres*, p. 43.
49. To Guibert, 1774, *Lettres*, p. 60.
50. To Guibert, May 30, 1773, *Lettres*, p. 9.
51. To Guibert, 1774, *Lettres*, p. 57.

V: CATHERINE THE GREAT

Catherine the Great, *Correspondence with Sir Charles Hanbury Williams* (translation Ilchester and Langford-Brooke).
Williams

Catherine the Great, Letters to Grimm, in *Collections of the Imperial Society of Russian History*, vol. XXIII.
Grimm

Catherine the Great, *Memoirs* (translation Katherine Anthony).
Memoirs

Waliszewski, I. L., *Le Roman d'une Impératrice*. Waliszewski

NOTES

1. *Memoirs*, p. 326.
2. *Memoirs of Poniatowski*, in Francis Gribble, *The Comedy of Catherine the Great*, p. 51.
3. Catherine, in *Memoirs*, edition A. Herzen (translation), p. 320.
4. *Memoirs*, p. 324.
5. Frances E. Willard, *Glimpses of Fifty Years*, p. 633.
6. *Correspondance de Ninon de Lenclos* (edition Colombey), p. 110.
7. November 6, 1764, in Pierre de Ségur, *Le Royaume de la Rue St. Honoré*, p. 437.
8. Grimm, p. 317.
9. Lucien Perey, *Figures du Temps Passé*, p. 206.
10. Waliszewski, p. 502.
11. Philip W. Sergeant, *The Courtships of Catherine the Great*, p. 286.
12. Grimm, p. 368.
13. Quoted in Dimitri Kobeko, *La Jeunesse d'un Tsar* (French translation), p. 15.
14. *Memoirs*, p. 212.
15. Princess Dashkov, *Memoirs* (English translation), vol. 1, p. 111.
16. Bernard Shaw, *Heartbreak House, Great Catherine, and Playlets of the War*, p. 134.
17. To Williams, August 12, 1756, Williams, p. 54.
18. To Williams, July 2, 1757, Williams, p. 283.
19. To Williams, August 9, 1756, Williams, p. 45.
20. To Grimm, August 11, 1778, Grimm, p. 96.
21. To Grimm, December 4, **1793**, Grimm, p. 587.
22. To Grimm, August 30, 1774, Grimm, p. 6.
23. To Grimm, August 27, 1794, Grimm, p. 606.
24. To Grimm, September 5, 1796, Grimm, p. 694.
25. In Pierre de Ségur, *Le Royaume de la Rue St. Honoré*, p. 432.
26. To Grimm, January 7, 1796, Grimm, p. 668.
27. In Edmond Scherer, *Études sur la Littérature Contemporaine*, vol. VII, p. 224.
28. *Ibid.*, p. 221.
29. Beaumont and Fletcher, *The Maid's Tragedy*, IV, 1.
30. In *Cambridge Modern History*, vol. VI, p. 696.
31. *Mémoire sur la Révolution*, in Charles de la Rivière, *La Russie au XVIII Siècle*, p. 375.

NOTES

32. In Lucien Perey, *Figures du Temps Passé*, p. 216.
33. To Meilhan, June, 1791, in La Rivière, *La Russie au XVIII Siècle*, p. 321.
34. To Grimm, November 30, 1778, Grimm, p. 116.
35. To Grimm, October 1, 1778, Grimm, p. 102.
36. To Grimm, March 5, 1785, Grimm, p. 327.
37. To Grimm, April 29, 1775, Grimm, p. 22.
38. To Grimm, 1775, Grimm, p. 33.
39. In Lucien Perey, *Figures du Temps Passé*, p. 156.
40. To Grimm, January 20, 1776, Grimm, p. 40.
41. To Williams, August 21, 1756, Williams, p. 70.
42. C. F. P. Masson, *Mémoires Secrètes sur la Russie*, p. 194.
43. Voltaire to Catherine, September, 1772, *Correspondance de Voltaire*, edition 1880, vol. XVI, p. 170.
44. In Francis Gribble, *The Comedy of Catherine the Great*, p. 51.

VI: GEORGE SAND

Amic, Henri, *George Sand*.   Amic
Karénine, Wladimir, *George Sand, Sa Vie et Ses Œuvres*, 4 vols.
                                                            Karénine
Pourtalès, Guy de, *Polonaise, The Life of Chopin* (translation)
                                                            Pourtalès
Sand, George et Gustave Flaubert, *Correspondance*.   Flaubert
Sand, George, *Correspondance*, 6 vols.   *Correspondance*
Sand, George, *Histoire de Ma Vie*, 4 vols.   *Histoire*
Sand, George, *Lettres à Alfred de Musset et à Sainte-Beuve*.
                                                    Lettres à Musset

1. In Sainte-Beuve, *Portraits Contemporains*, vol. I, p. 511.
2. Madame Juliette Adam, *Mes Sentiments et Nos Idées avant 1870*, p. 210.
3. To H. Amic, October 17, 1874, Amic, p. 62.
4. To Madame d'Agoult, November 1, 1835, *Correspondance*, vol. I, p. 316.
5. To Rocheblave, June 16, 1858, in Samuel Rocheblave, *George Sand et Sa Fille*, p. 195.
6. To Poncy, August 27, 1847, Karénine, vol. III, p. 583.

NOTES

7. Karénine, vol. III, p. 607.
8. Heine, *Lutezia*, chapter V.
9. Quoted in Karénine, vol. IV, p. 104.
10. To Grzymala, 1838, in Pourtalès, p. 147.
11. Amic, p. 106.
12. Sir William D'Avenant, *Gondibert*, book II, canto 7.
13. To Grzymala, 1838, in Pourtalès, p. 153.
14. To Musset (no date), *Lettres à Musset*, p. 75.
15. To Grzymala, 1838, in Pourtalès, p. 148.
16. To Musset (no date), *Lettres à Musset*, p. 88.
17. To Sainte-Beuve, July, 1833, in Paul Mariéton, *Une Histoire d'Amour*, p. 23.
18. To Grzymala, 1838, in Pourtalès, p. 147.
19. *Lélia*, vol. I, p. 66.
20. Speaking in the person of Jean Valreg, *La Daniella*, vol. I, p. 20.
21. January 17, 1869, Flaubert, p. 151.
22. To Boucoiran, February 12, 1831, *Correspondance*, vol. I, p. 158.
23. To Poncy, September 26, 1850, *Correspondance*, vol. III, p. 205.
24. February 13, 1834, in René Doumic, *George Sand*.
25. To Charles Edmond, January 9, 1858, *Correspondance*, vol. IV, p. 125.
26. Eugène Delacroix, *Journal*, October 17, 1853, vol. II, p. 250.
27. To Calamatta, May, 1837, *Correspondance*, vol. II, p. 74.
28. To Maurice Sand, February 26, 1870, *Correspondance*, vol. V, p. 366.
29. To Maurice Sand, March 2, 1864, *Correspondance*, vol. V, p. 19.
30. *Ibid.*
31. Letter of 1869, Rocheblave, *George Sand et Sa Fille*, p. 271.
32. Quoted in Article, *George Sand*, in *Encyclopædia Britannica*.
33. *Lélia*, vol. I, p. 104.
34. Matthew Arnold, essay on George Sand, in *Mixed Essays*.
35. To Mazzini, October 15, 1850, *Correspondance*, vol. III, p. 212.
36. October 25, 1872, Flaubert, p. 333.
37. George Sand, *Journal Intime*, May 7, 1847, p. 220.
38. To Alexandre Dumas fils, November 7, 1861, *Correspondance*, vol. IV, p. 296.

NOTES

39. December 18, 1875, Flaubert, p. 432.
40. *Journal Intime*, April 9, 1833, p. 148.
41. December 8, 1874, Flaubert, p. 413.
42. *Lélia*, vol. II, p. 160 (translated by Matthew Arnold in essay on George Sand).

VII: SARAH BERNHARDT

Bernhardt, Sarah, *The Art of the Theatre* (translation Stenning)
Art of Theatre
Bernhardt, Sarah, *Ma Double Vie, Mémoires*, 2 vols.
Mémoires
Claretie, Jules, *La Vie à Paris* (yearly chronicles).
Claretie, *Vie*
Claretie, Jules, *Souvenirs du Diner Bixio*.   Claretie, *Bixio*
Woon, Basil, *The Real Sarah Bernhardt* (from material supplied by Madame Pierre Berton).   Woon

1. Article in *Century Magazine*, July, 1923, vol. CVI, p. 470.
2. George Sand to Charles Edmond, November, 1837, *Correspondance de George Sand*, vol. VI, p. 176.
3. Claretie, *Vie*, 1880, p. 90.
4. Claretie, *Vie*, 1884, p. 450.
5. Maurice Baring, *Punch and Judy*, p. 35.
6. In Baring, *Punch and Judy*, p. 31.
7. *Autobiography of Joseph Jefferson*, p. 439.
8. *Art of Theatre*, p. 167.
9. *Mémoires*, vol. II, p. 68.
10. Quoted in Nina A. Kennard, *Mrs. Siddons*, p. 322.
11. Claretie, *Bixio*, p. 40.
12. Woon, p. 76.
13. Schurman, Impresario, *Les Étoiles en Voyage*, p. 140.
14. Claretie, *Bixio*, p. 35.
15. Claretie, *Vie*, 1883, p. 354.
16. Woon, p. 173.
17. *Ibid.*
18. Maurice Baring, *The Puppet Show of Memory*, p. 232.
19. Claretie, *Vie*, 1883, p. 352.

NOTES

20. Schurman, Impresario, *Les Étoiles en Voyage*, p. 102.
21. *Mémoires*, vol. II, p. 100.
22. Marie Colombier, *Les Voyages de Sarah Bernhardt en Amérique*, p. 153.
23. *Mémoires*, vol. II, p. 32.
24. Woon, p. 86.
25. Arsène Houssaye, *Les Confessions*, vol. IV, p. 403.
26. *Mémoires*, vol. II, p. 128.
27. *Art of Theatre*, p. 148.
28. Woon, p. 331.
29. *Mémoires*, vol. II, p. 231.
30. Woon, p. 354.
31. Claretie, *Vie*, 1884, p. 449.
32. *Mémoires*, vol. II, p. 72.
33. Claretie, *Vie*, 1884, p. 445.
34. Woon, p. 275.
35. *Ibid.*
36. Baring, *Punch and Judy*, p. 29.
37. *Mémoires*, vol. II, p. 39.
38. Francisque Sarcey, *Souvenirs d'Âge Mur*, p. 81.
39. Kennard, *Mrs. Siddons*, p. 92.
40. *Art of Theatre*, p. 158.
41. *Mémoires*, vol. I, p. 99.
42. *Autobiography of Joseph Jefferson*, p. 118.
43. Marie Colombier, *Mémoires de Sarah Barnum* (translation), p. 67.
44. Claretie, *Vie*, 1884, p. 446.
45. Clara Erskine Clement, *Charlotte Cushman*, p. 53.
46. In Henry Amic, *George Sand*, p. 147.
47. Woon, p. 105.
48. *Mémoires*, vol. I, p. 130.
49. Woon, p. 356.
50. Maurice Baring, *Punch and Judy*, p. 35.
51. Kennard, *Mrs. Siddons*, p. 327.
52. Claretie, *Vie*, 1884, p. 448.
53. *Mémoires*, vol. II, p. 12.

INDEX

INDEX

Albon, Comtesse d', mother of Mademoiselle de Lespinasse, 117

Alembert, Jean le Rond d', quoted on Mademoiselle de Lespinasse, 121, 124, 126; friend of Mademoiselle de Lespinasse, 127–29; his prominence as literary man, 133, 134; correspondence of Catherine the Great with, 179

Arnold, Matthew, Ninon de Lenclos quoted by, 29; quoted on Sophocles, 31

Aubigné, Agrippa d', grandfather of Madame de Maintenon, 35

Aubigné, Françoise d'. *See* Maintenon, Madame de

Austen, Jane, her interpretation of the human male, 228

Baring, Maurice, quoted on Sarah Bernhardt, 246, 254, 267, 278

Barnum, P. T., 259

Beauvilliers, Duchesse de, 102

Bernhardt, Madame, mother of Sarah, 251

Bernhardt, Maurice, son of Sarah, 252

Bernhardt, Sarah, chronology, 242; her motto, *Quand même*, 243, 277, 282; her career, 243; her influence on the art of acting, 244; her voice, 244, 245; her capacity for work, 245–47; her book on 'The Art of the Theatre,' 247, 248; her art, 248, 254, 255; her desire to create beauty, 248, 249; her intermingling of art and life, 250; her family relations, 251, 252; her love affairs, 252; her human interest, 255–57; her spiritual side, 256, 257; her extravagances, 257–61; publicity of, 259–62; her financial affairs, 262–65; as manageress, 265–67; her struggle with difficulties, 267; her physical weakness, 267–69; stage fright, 269, 270; her temper, 270, 271; relations with fellow actors, 271, 272; relations with managers, 272; relations with authors, 273; and critics, 274; attempted suicide of, 275, 276; her driving force, 276, 277; her ideal, 277, 278; her success on the stage, 278–82

Berton, Madame, on Sarah Bernhardt's career, 252, 254, 263

Boissier, Marie L. G., quoted on Madame de Maintenon, 42

Booth, Edwin, reference to, 280

Bossuet, Jacques Bénigne, opposed to ideas of Madame Guyon, 78, 104, 105

Boufflers, Madame de, friend of Mademoiselle de Lespinasse, 120

Brinon, Madame de, head of Saint-Cyr, and Madame de Maintenon, 62

Burr, Aaron, and Catherine the Great, 197

Butler, Sarah, her letters, 142

Caraccioli, and Madame de Lespinasse, 127

Catherine the Great, chronology, 156; her career, 157; epitaph of, 157, 158; her love affairs, 158–66; her household management, 166–68; her money affairs, 168; her treatment of servants, 169; her pets, 170; her family relations, 170, 171; her human interests, 171–74; her ambition, 175, 176; becomes ruler of Russia, 176, 177; her enjoyment of rule, 177, 178, 180,

INDEX

INDEX

for religious emotion, 10; a creature of this world, 10, 11; her beauty, 12; her lovers, 13–16; love not taken seriously by, 14, 17; her story 'La Coquette Vengée,' 16; insisted on masculine privileges and duties for women, 18; her loyalty and fidelity, 18, 22, 23; father's deathbed speech to, 19; as a mother, 19; with her domestics, 19; in financial concerns, 20–22; her social grace and charm, 23; her human sympathy, 24; her old age, 24–32; correspondence with Saint-Évremond, 27–29; verses written by, 31; an epitaph for, 32; her evidence concerning Madame de Maintenon, 65; quotation from, 166, 197

Lespinasse, Julie de, chronology, 116; her career, 117, 118; her sufferings, 118, 119; her family difficulties, 119, 120; her female friends, 120; relations with Madame du Deffand, 121–23 (cf. 118); her Salon, 122, 123, 125, 133, 140; her charm, 123; her attitude toward money, 124, 125; her tact, 125–27; her attraction, 126–28; and D'Alembert, 127–29; her intellectual force, 129–32; her interest in literature, 132; takes part in the politico-literary game, 133–35; her æsthetic interest, 135–37; had no enjoyment of nature, 137; had no interest in religion, 138, 139; her lovers, 139–42; record of her sufferings, 142–53

Ligne, Prince de, quoted on Catherine the Great, 182, 189, 193

Louis XIV, King, and Madame de Maintenon, 36, 54, 56, 66–68

Love, elements in, 112

Loyola, Ignatius, blend of philanthropy and self-assertion in, 99

Maine, Duke of, 63, 68

Maintenon, Madame de, friend of Ninon de Lenclos, 20, 23; chronology, 34; her career, 35–37; her instinct to advance, 37; disclaims ambition, 37, 38; longs for repose, 39; her duty to save the King, 40, 50; her intellect, 41, 42; an educator, 42; unattracted by abstract interests of intellectual life, 42, 43; her letters, 43, 44; her keenness, 44, 45; analyzes own faults, 45, 46; her conversation, 47; her desire to conciliate, 48; her charm, 49, 50; becomes Queen in all but name, 51; how she used her power, 52–57; her school at Saint-Cyr, 57, 58; was feminine in her tastes, 59; her attitude toward servants, 59; dress, 60; health, 60; her view of money, 61; as to her human relations, 62; love of children, 63; letters to brother, 64; her attitude toward sex affection, 64–66; relations to King, 66–68; retires to Saint-Cyr, 68; her religion, 68–72; her reasonableness, 70–72; her lack of attraction, 72, 73; and Madame Guyon, 78, 102

Mamonov, favorite of Catherine the Great, 160, 180

Marmontel, Jean François, and Mademoiselle de Lespinasse, 127

Masochism, 111

Meilhac (Henri) and Halévy (Ludovic), their 'Frou-Frou,' 273

Mérimée, Prosper, lover of George Sand, 205

Molière, J. B., read his plays to Ninon de Lenclos, 7

Montaigne, M. E. de, quoted, 30

Montespan, Madame de, and Madame de Maintenon, 36, 50, 62

Montrose, Marquis of, quoted, 282

Moody, D. L., blend of philanthropy and self-assertion in, 99, 101, 109

Mora, Marquis de, and Mademoiselle de Lespinasse, 140, 141, 143, 149

Musset, Alfred de, lover of George Sand, 205, 216

Mysticism, elements in, 110–13; rapture and ecstasy of, 114

302

INDEX

Noailles, Cardinal de, and Madame de Maintenon, 63, 70, 71

Orleans, Duchess of, 56
Orlov, Gregory, lover of Catherine the Great, 160
Orlovs, the, 176

Pagello, Dr., lover of George Sand, 205, 216
Panin, and Catherine the Great, 176
Paris, Archbishop of, letter of Madame de Maintenon to, 38
Pascal, Blaise, quoted, 113
Paul, Emperor, 159, 170
Peter III, of Russia, married to Catherine, 157, 158; character, 158, 159; becomes Emperor, 176; murder of, 177
Poniatowski, lover of Catherine the Great, 159, 160; quoted on Catherine the Great, 196
Potemkin, Prince, favorite of Catherine the Great, 160, 178; letter to, 164
Pugachev rebellion, 177, 186

Quietist controversy, 104

Racine, Jean Baptiste, Madame de Maintenon writes to, 43
Richardson, Samuel, admired by Mademoiselle de Lespinasse, 132
Richepin, Jean, and Sarah Bernhardt, 273
Roosevelt, Theodore, and Sarah Bernhardt, 266, 277
Rostand, Edmond, and Sarah Bernhardt, 274, 279
Rousseau, Jean Jacques, admired by Mademoiselle de Lespinasse, 132

Sadism, 111
Saint Catherine of Genoa, saintliness of, 98; her use of terms borrowed from sexual love, 110
Saint-Cyr, Madame de Maintenon's

convent at, 57, 58; Madame Guyon's doctrines in, 102
Saint-Évremond, Seigneur de, correspondence with Ninon de Lenclos, 27–29
Saint Francis of Sales, blend of philanthropy and self-assertion in, 99
Saint John of the Cross, quoted, 91
Saint-Simon, quoted on Ninon de Lenclos, 26; referred to, on Madame de Maintenon, 44, 60, 62
Saint Teresa, her use of terms borrowed from sexual love, 110
Sainte-Beuve, Charles A., his analysis of character of Saint-Évremond, 27; quoted on old age, 30; quoted with reference to Madame de Maintenon, 51, 63; quoted on Mademoiselle de Lespinasse, 117; referred to on Catherine the Great, 161, 165, 166; on George Sand, 232
Saintliness, two types of, 98, 99
Salons, 122, 133
Sand, George, chronology, 200; career, 201–06; her novels, 204; her lovers, 205; her idealism, 206–39; her Autobiography, 208; her correspondence with Flaubert, 211, 212; her love affairs, 212–17; her mother-instinct, 213, 216, 217; her writing, 219–21; her treatment of ambition, 221–23; her attitude toward money, 223–25; her playwriting, 225; her artistic achievement, 226, 227; her character-drawing, 227; her heroines, 227, 228; her heroes, 228, 229; her style, 229, 230; her nature-descriptions, 230, 231; her interest in politics, 232; her mental activity, 234; her attitude toward suicide, 235; her spiritual life, 236–39; and Sarah Bernhardt, 245, 275, 276
Sandeau, Jules, lover of George Sand, 205
Sarcey, Francisque, quoted on Sarah Bernhardt, 247, 269

INDEX